SIR WALTER SCOTT

1771-1971

A BICENTENARY EXHIBITION

EDINBURGH

ORGANISED BY

THE COURT OF SESSION, THE FACULTY OF ADVOCATES

AND

THE NATIONAL LIBRARY OF SCOTLAND

In The Parliament House, Edinburgh. 15th August – 11th September

1971

Designed by Graphic Partners, Edinburgh
and printed in Scotland for Her Majesty's Stationery Office
by Robert MacLehose & Co. Ltd, Glasgow
Dd 243228
© Crown copyright 1971
SBN 902220 04 7

CONTENTS

PARLIAMENT HOUSE

THE purpose of this exhibition is to show something of Scott's life, work, background and influence in the context of the building which was the focus of his professional life, and whose ancient atmosphere and traditions inspired some of his best-loved writings. The building is an integral part of the exhibition and some knowledge of its history and fabric helps towards an understanding of the part it played in Scott's life and writings.

The Parliament House dates from the seventeenth century—that troubled period of Scottish history between the Union of the Crowns under King James VI and I in 1603 and the Union of the Parliaments under Queen Anne in 1707.

When King James went south to claim the crown of England, he left behind him an unruly country whose capital had none of the buildings normally associated with efficient administration. Edinburgh had no House of Parliament, no Government offices, and no Law Courts. Only St Giles' Cathedral and the Old Tolbooth ('The Heart of Midlothian', now demolished) were available for these purposes. By contrast, England was governed with relative efficiency from the Palaces of Westminster and Whitehall in London.

When King Charles I returned to Scotland, he was appalled to find the seat of national government confined to cramped and undignified quarters in the Cathedral or the Tolbooth. He therefore ordered the Town Council of Edinburgh to build a new house for his Parliament and his Lords of Session.

The site selected for the building was the steeply-sloping old graveyard of St. Giles's, running down from the High Street to the Cowgate. After considerable delays, the new Parliament House was completed in 1639. The building is L-shaped, consisting of two great halls, one above the other, which provided accommodation for the Parliament, and an annexe to house the Supreme Court and government offices.

The Court suffered greatly during the troubles of the seventeenth century: 'Long cessation for near three years by reason of the troubles in the country', reads a contemporary law report after 1639. The College of Justice was in abeyance for eleven years while Cromwell's 'Commissioners' usurped the Lords of Session, but after the Restoration of the College in 1661 the hall was restored to its former state. Until the Union with England in 1707 the building was occupied by the Parliament (known as the Estates), the Privy Council of Scotland, and the Supreme Court (known as the Court of Session). After the Union the first two ceased to exist, but the building remained (as it is to this day) the seat of the Court of Session, whose continued existence was guaranteed by the Treaty of Union.

For much of his life as an advocate, Scott was one of the Clerks of the Court of Session, and his professional life was therefore passed in a building which represented a living and continuous link with the days of Scottish independence. The history and traditions of the Parliament House, and the habits of thought and expression of his legal colleagues there, were an essential part of his background, and several scenes from the novels were set there. Scott compared its 'stifling fumes' with the 'sweet air of Tweedside', but the Parliament House also contributed to the building of Abbotsford, for Scott secured an old stone gate from the Parliament House to ornament his country house and provide another link with the old building he loved so well.

Buildings like the Parliament House and Laigh Hall helped to kindle in the young Walter Scott a deep and romantic appreciation of the merits of Scottish history. Likewise his own works established in a later Scotland a climate of opinion that looked back with interest and acceptance to the themes which Scott took as sources of inspiration. This opening section illustrates the spirit of historical romanticism which was so important a part of Sir Walter Scott's legacy to Scotland.

1 (detail)

THE LAIGH HALL

5 Sir Walter Scott
Sir Henry Raeburn. Oil, 1808.
His Grace the Duke of Buccleuch

THE Laigh, or lower, Hall is the oldest part of the building. Shortly after its construction, it is said to have been used as a stable by Oliver Cromwell, and as a prison. After the Restoration of King Charles II in 1660, the Hall became the meeting-place of the Scottish Privy Council, which mercilessly tortured and condemned the leaders of the Covenanting party, including the Earl of Argyll.

This painting—the definitive portrait of Scott in his prime—was commissioned by Thomas Constable the publisher in 1808 and was bought from him by the Duke of Buccleuch in 1826. Hermitage Castle, in Liddesdale, is in the background and the dog Camp lies at his master's feet. In 1809, after his quarrel with Constable, Scott commissioned from Raeburn the version, with alterations, which now hangs at Abbotsford.

After the Union, the Hall was used to house the records of Scotland and the steadily-growing Advocates' Library. At the end of the eighteenth century, the records were moved to Adam's Register House, but the Hall remained a library. In 1925 the Faculty of Advocates presented all but its legal books and manuscripts to the nation, and the books were eventually moved to the National Library of Scotland. In 1965, the bookcases were removed, and the Hall restored to its present state.

As the meeting-place of the Privy Council, the Hall is the scene of the trial in *Old Mortality*, chapter 34. Here, in this 'ancient dark Gothic room', Henry Morton was granted his pardon on condition of permanent exile, and Ephraim Macbriar faced the Duke of Lauderdale with defiant jests:

' "Ay, but there are some things which must go before an easy death, if you continue obstinate," said Lauderdale, and rung a small silver bell which was placed before him on the table.

'A dark crimson curtain, which covered a sort of niche, or Gothic recess in the wall, rose at the signal, and displayed the public executioner, a tall grim, and hideous man, having an oaken table before him, on which lay thumb-screws, and an iron case, called the Scottish boot, used in those tyrannical days to torture accused persons. Morton, who was unprepared for this ghastly apparition, started when the curtain arose, but Macbriar's nerves were more firm. He gazed upon the horrible apparatus with much composure; and if a touch of nature called the blood from his cheek for a second, resolution sent it back to his brow with greater energy.

' "Do you know who that man is?" said Lauderdale, in a low, stern voice, almost sinking into a whisper.

' "He is, I suppose," replied Macbriar, "the infamous executioner of your bloodthirsty commands upon the persons of God's people. He and you are equally beneath my regard; and, I bless God, I no more fear what he can inflict than what you can command. . . ." '

The members of the Privy Council at this time were the 'set of ghastly revellers' in 'Wandering Willie's Tale' (*Redgauntlet*, letter XI)—'the fierce Middleton, and the dissolute Rothes, and the crafty Lauderdale; and Dalyell, with his bald head and his beard to his girdle; and Earlshall, with Cameron's blude on his hand; and wild Bonshaw, that tied blessed Mr Cargill's limbs till the blude sprung; and Dunbarton Douglas, the twice-turned traitor baith to country and king. There was the Bluidy Advocate Mackenzie, who for all his worldly wit and wisdom, had been to the rest as a god. And there was Claverhouse, as beautiful as when he lived, with his long dark curled locks streaming down over his laced buff-coat, and his left hand always on his right spule-blade, to hide the wound that the silver bullet had made. He sat apart from them all, and looked at them with a melancholy, haughty countenance; while the rest hallooed and sung, and laughed that the room rang.'

Another famous literary scene took place in this Hall. When Scott was two years old, Boswell took Dr Johnson on his tour of the Hebrides. The tour started in Edinburgh and on 16 August 1773 Johnson visited the Laigh Hall. 'I was pleased to behold Dr Samuel Johnson rolling about in this old magazine of antiquities. There was by this time a pretty numerous circle of us standing upon him . . . I here began to indulge old Scottish sentiments and expressed a warm regret that by our Union with England, we were no more—our independent kingdom was lost. JOHNSON: "Sir, never talk of your independency, who could let your Queen remain twenty years in captivity, and then be put to death without even a pretence of justice, without your ever attempting to rescue her; and such a Queen too as every man of any gallantry of spirit would have sacrificed his life for." '

SCOTT'S EDINBURGH
The Changing City

EDINBURGH, even in Scott's time, was a city of dramatic contrasts. Its centre was still the High Street, but the better class of citizen had moved to 'the New Town'—the elegant streets and squares to the north, to which the North Bridge and the earthen Mound gave access.

The New Town was largely created within Scott's lifetime. James Craig's plan was finally accepted and the first feus in St Andrews Square let only four years before he was born. By the time of his marriage in 1797 development had moved west as far as Castle Street, where Scott bought his first house; and by the time of his death most of what we now know as New Town Edinburgh was complete. He saw the opening of most of the great public buildings—the Assembly Rooms in George Street, the Royal Institution building at the foot of the Mound (now the Royal Scottish Academy), the Edinburgh Academy in Henderson Row (of which he was one of the Governors) and the new High School in Regent Terrace, which replaced the old school in which he himself had been educated.

The bold and imaginative plans of Craig and his successors brought into existence not only a new town but a new way of life. Scott and his generation enjoyed a style of living which uniquely combined elegance and intimacy. Within a mile of Scott's house in Castle Street lived almost all his friends. Edinburgh's dinner parties and supper parties were famous, and the guests were close enough to walk unless the weather was bad. It was a civilized, well-to-do society of gentlemen, many of them advocates and many of them known to each other from their school and college days. It was far removed from the noisy, crowded Edinburgh into which Scott had been born, and from the Edinburgh of the Porteous Riots or Prince Charles's Court at Holyrood.

To that world, however—the Edinburgh which he celebrated in his novels—Scott returned each day. As the Clerks' Coach wound its way up the earthen Mound to the Parliament House, Scott was transported from the New Town to the old world. He worked, until they were replaced by a new building in 1808, in the very courts where Effie Deans had stood her trial; within a stone's throw of the 'Heart of Midlothian', the town jail; almost within sight of the palace from which Prince Charles had set off for Prestonpans. It is small wonder that the theme of many of his novels—for example, *Waverley*, *Rob Roy* and *Redgauntlet*—is so often the change of the old ways into the new. It was visible all around him in substantial stone and lime.

In his lifetime Scott saw many of the traditional national ways disappear. The law was reformed, and Scott mistrusted the motives of the reformers, which he feared were dictated by 'Anglomania—a rage of imitating English forms and practice'. Scotland's distinctive accent was being rubbed away by constant contact of all kinds with the more powerful southern neighbour. 'Scotch was a language,' Scott wrote to Constable in 1822, 'which we have heard spoken by the learnd and the wise & witty & the accomplishd and which had not a trace of vulgarity in it but on the contrary sounded rather graceful and genteel. . . . But that is all gone & the remembrance will be drownd with us the elders of this existing generation.' It was to preserve some memory of the Scotland that was now passing away for ever that Scott wrote his first and his best novels.

Scott was fascinated by the past, and yet he was a true son of the Enlightenment. His novels celebrate the old heroic virtues of loyalty and courage even against hopeless odds, but they admit that the old world has gone forever: the future lies with Bailie Jarvie and Alan Fairford, not with Rob Roy and Redgauntlet. Abbotsford was filled with antiquarian treasures—and lit by gas.

The maps and views of the time illustrate the process of expansion and change in Edinburgh over the period of Scott's lifetime. Among the drawings are some by Scott's friend James Skene of Rubislaw, with whom at one time he contemplated producing a volume of illustrations of the vanishing old town with descriptive notes. In Scott's lifetime too the first steps were taken to re-house the records of Scotland, and the building of Register House was not only an undertaking of unparalleled size in terms of the city's buildings but also a milestone in the resurrection of Scottish history.

7

8

SCOTT'S FAMILY

10 Sir Walter Scott

James Saxon. Oil, 1805.
Scottish National Portrait Gallery

This portrait was commissioned by
Scott's wife in 1805, and was her favourite
representation of her husband. It was
engraved as the frontispiece to the first
edition of *The Lady of the Lake* in 1810.
Saxon's portrait of Lady Scott hangs at
Abbotsford.

11 Walter Scott, W.S.

Robert Harvie. Oil.
Mrs Maxwell-Scott of Abbotsford

Eldest son of Robert Scott of Sandy-
Knowe and father of Sir Walter. He was
a hard-working, devout, and punctilious
Writer to the Signet, with an extensive
legal practice and none of his son's
literary interests. 'According to every
account', Lockhart wrote of him, 'he was
a most just, honourable, conscientious
man.' Although he lived in Edinburgh, he
remained a lover of his native Borders,
and carried on much of his business in
Roxburghshire. Walter Scott senior is
immortalized in *Redgauntlet*, where he
appears as 'the good old-fashioned man
of method', Saunders Fairford.

12 Anne Rutherford, Mrs Scott

Robert Harvie. Oil.
Mrs Maxwell-Scott of Abbotsford

Sir Walter's mother was the eldest
daughter of Dr John Rutherford, Professor of Medicine in the University of
Edinburgh. She was intelligent and well-
educated, although, as Lockhart says, 'by
no means comely'. Sir Walter was the
ninth of her twelve children, of whom the
first six died in infancy.

BORDER BACKGROUND
Family and Countryside

Scott was proud of his 'Berwickshire *burr*' and of his Border ancestry. He came of Border stock; he spent much of his childhood at Sandy-Knowe and Kelso; he was for more than thirty years Sheriff of Selkirkshire; and he built Abbotsford, inevitably, beside the Tweed.

'Every Scottishman has a pedigree', he wrote in the fragment of auto-biography which became the first chapter of Lockhart's *Life*. 'It is a national prerogative as unalienable as his pride and his poverty.' His own pedigree was romantic enough, 'no bad genealogy for a Border minstrel'. He could trace his descent on his father's side back through the Walter Scott known as 'Beardie' (because he would not shave until the Stuarts were restored), to Auld Watt of Harden and his wife Mary, 'the Flower of Yarrow'. There was a connection too with the Haliburtons, and on his mother's side with the family of Swinton.

The ties of blood were reinforced by those of early association. After the illness (probably polio) which left him lame from the age of eighteen months, he was sent to the country to recuperate, and it was 'at Sandy-Knowe, in the residence of my paternal grandfather', he wrote later, that he had 'the first consciousness of existence'. His imagination was early fired by Smailholm, the old tower which stood near the farm, and by the tales told by his grand-mother and his aunts 'of old, unhappy, far-off things, and battles long ago'. Many of the ballads which he was later to collect in the *Minstrelsy of the Scottish Border* Scott knew by heart before he could read.

To Sandy-Knowe and Kelso he returned frequently during his boyhood and youth—to the farm, to his aunt's cottage in Kelso, or to Rosebank, where his uncle lived. During one of his longer visits, in 1783, he attended Kelso Grammar School for a time, under the Rev. Launcelot Whale (who is thought to have contributed some features to Dominie Sampson), and it was there that he made the acquaintance of James Ballantyne. The border land-scape gave him a strong feeling for natural beauty. He recalled that its historical and legendary associations 'gave to my admiration a feeling of reverence, which at times made my heart feel too big for its bosom'.

In 1792, the summer of his admission to the Faculty of Advocates, Scott made the first of his 'raids', as he liked to call them, up Liddesdale in search of antiquities and ballads. These holiday excursions in the company of Robert Shortreed, the Sheriff-Substitute of Roxburghshire, were repeated for seven successive summers. Their memorial is the *Minstrelsy*, but their effect was felt far beyond that first publication. 'He was makin' himsell' a' the time,' Shortreed told Lockhart; and indeed the influence of those summers and of the people he met in a district where no wheeled carriage had ever been until Scott himself took a gig there in 1798 is to be traced in the best of his Scottish novels.

On 16 December 1799, through the influence of the head of his clan, the Duke of Buccleuch, Scott was appointed Sheriff of Selkirkshire. The post brought him a salary of £300 a year; the duties, in a rural and generally (with the exception of the poaching) law-abiding district, were light. It gave him time to write, and an excuse for spending part of every year in the Borders.

From 1804 until 1811 he rented Ashestiel, on the south bank of the Tweed near Galashiels, from his cousin James Russell, who was serving in India. In that comfortable, unpretentious house, Scott spent some of the happiest months of his life, and he wrote there the poems which first made him famous—*The Lay of the Last Minstrel, Marmion*, and *The Lady of the Lake*—as well as the early chapters of *Waverley*. Had Russell been willing to sell, Scott would have stayed there; instead, he embarked on his ambitious schemes of building and improvement at Abbotsford.

13 Sir Walter Scott, 2nd Baronet
a Oil, b Photograph
Mrs Maxwell-Scott of Abbotsford

Scott adored his elder son (later the second Sir Walter). 'He has good sense and the most perfect good temper,' he told Lady Louisa Stuart, 'bel cavalier beau sabreur a very good husband to his little wife.' But 'Don Whiskerandos', as Scott nicknamed him, was also obstinate and at times uncivil, and although seriously devoted to his military duties in the 15th Hussars he was not a stranger to the gaming-table.

In 1825 he married Sir Adam Ferguson's niece, Jane Jobson, a dull girl with an attractive fortune and an estate in Fife.

14

14 Anne Scott

William Nicholson.
Water-colour, signed, 1818.
Mrs Maxwell-Scott of Abbotsford

Scott's good-looking younger daughter kept house for him after Lady Scott's death, and died unmarried in 1833. She gave free play to a satirical and irreverent wit, but at the time of the family distress Scott found, as Lockhart had done, 'what a strong fund of sound sense lies under the disguize of her ladyship's persifflage'.

15 Sophia Scott, Mrs Lockhart

William Nicholson.
Water-colour, signed, 1818.
Mrs Maxwell-Scott of Abbotsford

'Sophia Scott is a remarkable girl, about eighteen or nineteen, with great simplicity and naturalness of manners, not a remarkable degree of talent and yet full of enthusiasm; with tact in everything, a lover of old ballads, a Jacobite; and, in short, in all respects, such a daughter as Scott ought to have and ought to be proud of.' So wrote George Ticknor, an American visitor to Scotland.

Sophia married John Gibson Lockhart in 1820 and had three children. She was a devoted wife and a doting mother to Johnnie, Walter and Charlotte.

16 John Gibson Lockhart

Sir Francis Grant. Oil.
Scottish National Portrait Gallery

Scott's son-in-law and biographer was closer to him in many ways than were his own children, and when Lockhart was appointed editor of the *Quarterly Review* in 1826 and moved to London, Scott felt the loss of the one member of his family with whom he could discuss literary matters. Despite the withdrawn appearance and satirical eye, Lockhart was a kind man to those close to him—an excellent husband and father, and assiduous in writing to his father-in-law when political affairs in London took an interesting turn. He is remembered now less for his early squibs in *Blackwood's Magazine* than for his enormous *Life of Scott*, which was published by Cadell in 1837–8.

17 Johnnie Lockhart

Margaret Carpenter. Oil, signed.
Mrs Maxwell-Scott of Abbotsford

'O my God, that poor delicate child, so clever, so animated, yet holding by this earth with so fearfully slight a tenure— Never out of his mother's thoughts, almost never out of his father's arms when he has but a single moment to give to anything.'—*Journal*, 2 December 1825.

John Hugh Lockhart—the 'Hugh Littlejohn' for whom Scott wrote his *Tales of a Grandfather*—was the eldest son of Sophia and John Lockhart. He suffered throughout his short life from a disease of the spine.

18   Charlotte Lockhart
Josiah Slater. Pencil with colour, signed, 1833.
Mrs Maxwell-Scott of Abbotsford

Scott's grand-daughter, whom he nicknamed 'Whippety-Stourie' after the fairy in a Scottish tale. As a baby Anne Scott thought her 'very like Sophia' with 'most engaging manners'. Alone of Scott's grand-children she married and brought up a family: the Maxwell-Scotts of Abbotsford are descended from her and her husband James Robert Hope-Scott.

19   Pedigree of the Scott Family
Partly in the hand of Sir Walter Scott.
Lord Polwarth

SCOTT'S COUNTRY

20   Border Scenes
Topographical drawings: Scott's cottage at Lasswade; Smailholm Tower; Melrose Abbey—the exterior; Melrose Abbey—the interior.
National Gallery of Scotland

21   Roadside Scene
Walter Geikie. Oil.
National Gallery of Scotland

22   Robert Shortreed
Silhouette portrait.
National Gallery of Scotland

23   Chiefswood
Tom Scott. Water-colour, 1892.
Mrs Wheeler-Carmichael

24 Sir Walter Scott

Sir Henry Raeburn. Oil, 1822.
Scottish National Portrait Gallery

The later Raeburn portrait of Scott contrasts with the 1808 painting, for it is very much the apotheosis of Scott at the height of his fame. Writing to Lord Montagu from Abbotsford on 27 March 1812, Scott says: 'I will contribute the head you wish to the halls of Ditton. I know no place where the substance has been so happy and therefore where the shadow may be so far well placed. . . . I will arrange with Raeburn when I return to Edinburgh in May.' Raeburn himself died in July 1823.

25 James Hogg (1770–1835)

William Nicholson. Oil.
Mr William Nichol

Scott first met 'the Ettrick Shepherd' when he was collecting ballads for the *Minstrelsy*. As a farmer, Hogg was not successful; as a writer, he earned a substantial reputation from his *Confessions of a Justified Sinner*, his numerous articles for *Blackwood's Magazine*, and from his poetry (which is now less highly regarded than it was at the time). His *Domestic Manners of Sir Walter Scott* well illustrates his (perhaps pardonable) self-importance.

Lockhart tells the story of Hogg's first visit to Castle Street, when, finding Lady Scott unwell, he stretched himself out at full length on another sofa, explaining afterwards that he thought he 'could never do wrong to copy the lady of the house'.

26 Henry Mackenzie (1745–1831)

Colvin Smith. Oil.
Scottish National Portrait Gallery

The grand old man of Scottish letters, universally known after the title of his famous work as 'the Man of Feeling', was an early encourager of Scott and a stimulus to his study of German literature. 'No man is less known from his writings,' Scott wrote of him at the age of eighty. 'We would suppose a retired, modest, somewhat affected man with a white handkerchief and a sigh ready for every sentiment. No such thing. H.M. is as alert as a contracting tailor's needle in every sort of business, a politician and a sportsman, shoots and fishes in a sort even to this day, and is the life of the company with anecdote and fun.'—*Journal*.

27 Lord Byron (1788–1824)

W. E. West. Oil.
Scottish National Portrait Gallery

It was the success of Byron's narrative poems that turned Scott towards the novel in 1814, although they did not meet until the following year, when John Murray the publisher brought them together in London. Differing over religion and

politics, they nonetheless became friends. Byron presented Scott with a silver urn of Greek bones and dedicated his *Cain* to him; in *Don Juan* he called him 'the Ariosto of the North' and in a private letter 'certainly the most wonderful writer of the day'. Scott admired 'his generosity of Spirit as well as purse and his utter contempt of all the affectations of literature', and believed him to be 'in many respects "Le fanfaron des vices qu'il n'avoit pas" '.—*Journal*.

28 Susan Ferrier (1782–1854)

A. Edouart. Silhouette.
Scottish National Portrait Gallery

Susan Ferrier was the daughter of Scott's friend James Ferrier, a fellow Clerk of Session. Scott admired her novels—*Marriage, The Inheritance* and *Destiny*—and her talent as a conversationalist, 'simple, full of humour, and exceedingly ready at repartee'.

Scott's friendships were not confined to one circle. As an advocate he belonged to that Edinburgh aristocracy which he calls in *Redgauntlet* the 'noblesse of the robe'. As a writer he had friends among the book-sellers as well as among literary celebrities of his time. As a scholar and antiquarian he carried on a correspondence with acquaintances from all over the British Isles and beyond. As a man of genius, and as a poet popular as no poet is today, he was accepted in the great world of Court and Cabinet. No man in Scotland knew more people, or more kinds of people, for his acquaintances ranged from the peer to the ploughman, from the King and the Duke of Wellington to the families of the cottagers on the Abbotsford estate. He was accessible to them all, even when heavily pressed by literary work in his study at Abbotsford.

Among lawyers he was much at home. The Clerks of Session were a brotherhood within the brotherhood, who shared 'ten minutes either of sense or fun' in the Clerks' Coach which took them up the Mound each morning. Scott had been at school and college with many of those who became judges and senior advocates, and although the Law was for him mainly the means of providing a comfortable salary, the leading lawyers were the intimate friends of his social circle.

John and James Ballantyne, Archibald Constable, and latterly Robert Cadell (Constable's junior partner) were business associates who were also friends. They dined with Scott and he with them, and their visits to Abbotsford combined business and pleasure.

Literary friendships made no particular appeal to Scott, and he scorned the imaginary consequences of literary people who walk with their noses in the air'. But of course he knew the great writers of the day. While still a schoolboy he had met Burns at the house of Professor Ferguson; he dined in company with Coleridge in London; he knew Southey, Maria Edgeworth, George Crabbe, Fanny Burney, Fenimore Cooper, Washington Irving, and the young Disraeli, James Hogg, Allan Cunningham and 'Christopher North'. The writers he liked best were those whom he also admired as people: Byron, with whom he struck up a warm friendship in 1815; Wordsworth, whose plain, straightforward character appealed to him where Coleridge's metaphysical eccentricities merely amused him; Susan Ferrier, whose father was a fellow Clerk of Session; Tom Moore, the Irish poet, who was content to be a good-humoured fellow rather than a literary lion.

Scott's closest friend in high political circles was Lord Melville, his old schoolfellow, for many years First Lord of the Admiralty, but he knew Canning, Wellington and Peel well. In London, especially in his later years, he was fêted by all. King George IV, who had always admired the novels, commanded him down to spend the day at Windsor. He dined time after time with members of the Cabinet, with wits and bishops, painters and men of letters. The attentions he was shown pleased him, but the homelier fare of his intimates in Edinburgh pleased him better; and to both he vastly pre-ferred Abbotsford, where he had his family, his treasures, and his trees.

9   Robert Burns (1759–96)
. Miers. Silhouette.
Scottish National Portrait Gallery

Scott was fifteen when he met Burns at Professor Ferguson's house and attracted his attention by identifying some lines of verse by Langthorne. His recollection of Burns was that 'his countenance was more massive than it looks in any of the portraits' and that his eye 'literally glowed' as he spoke. Scott was fond of quoting from his poetry: 'Long life to thy fame and peace to thy soul, Rob Burns. When I want to express a senti-ment which I feel strongly, I find the phrase in Shakespeare or thee.'—*Journal*.

30   Joanna Baillie (1762–1851)
Mary Ann Knight. Drawing.
Scottish National Portrait Gallery

Scott was introduced to Joanna Baillie by Sotheby in 1806. He corresponded with her for the rest of his life, and visited her at Hampstead whenever the chance arose. No doubt he rather overestimated his fellow-countrywoman's poetical and dramatic talents. Her *Plays on the Passions* and *Family Legend* (for which Scott wrote a prologue) are never performed and seldom read nowadays. She and her sister lived to a great age, genial and hospitable to the end.

31   Allan Cunningham (1784–1842)
J. J. Penston. Drawing.
Scottish National Portrait Gallery

'Honest Allan—a leal true Scotsman of the old cast, A man of genius besides. . . .' —*Journal*, 14 November 1826.

Cunningham was a stonemason from Nithsdale who became Clerk of Works to Chantrey the sculptor. He is now remembered for his poetry. Scott looked upon ' "A Wet Sheet and a Flowing Sea" as among the best songs going'; he was personally very kind to him and procured a cadetship for his son.

32   Samuel Taylor Coleridge (1772–1834)
Robert Hancock. Drawing.
National Portrait Gallery, London

'That extraordinary man Coleridge.'—*Journal*, 22 April 1828.

Scott and Coleridge were not close friends but they met occasionally at Sotheby's dinner-parties. Scott's description of Coleridge's behaviour on one such occasion is recorded by Mrs Hughes in her *Recollections*:

'After eating, as never Man eat before, and drinking with every person with whom he could possibly make an excuse to take wine, thrusting himself besides as Thirdsman whenever he saw two people drinking together; at last, when the cheese was brought on the table, he began in a most oracular tone, and without the least thing having been said which could have led to it, an Oration which lasted three quarters of an hour on the Samo-Thracian mysteries.'

Scott admired and often quoted his poetry, in particular *Christabel*, to which *The Lay of the Last Minstrel* is indebted.

33   William Wordsworth (1770–1850)
Robert Hancock. Drawing.
National Portrait Gallery, London

'A better or more sensible man I do not know than W. W.' was Scott's estimate in 1828 of the man he had by then known for twenty-five years. He never understood, however, why Wordsworth continued to write poetry which was 'too subtle and metaphysical in the idea, and too blunt in the expression', when 'he could be popular if he would'. Scott and Wordsworth were deeply attracted to each other. They first met in 1803 when Wordsworth and his sister Dorothy were on a tour in Scotland, and Wordsworth's 'Yarrow Revisited' was inspired by his last visit to Abbotsford a few days before Scott set off for the Mediterranean in the vain quest for renewed health.

34   Thomas Moore (1779–1852)
Engraving.
Scottish National Portrait Gallery

The Irish poet visited Scotland in the autumn of 1825, and Scott took to him as to a kindred spirit: 'There is a manly frankness and perfect ease and good

36

38

breeding about him which is delightful. Not the least touch of the poet or the pedant . . . we have both seen the world too widely and too well not to contemn in our souls the imaginary consequence of literary people who walk with their noses in the air.'—*Journal*, 22 November 1825.

Moore later dedicated his *Life of Byron* to Scott.

35 Matthew Lewis (1775–1818)
H. W. Pickersgill. Oil.
National Portrait Gallery, London

The Monk, which appeared in 1795, enjoyed an exaggerated success, and Scott was flattered by the attentions of Lewis in Edinburgh in 1798 and by his invitation to contribute to his *Tales of Wonder*. It was through Lewis, too, that his translation of Goethe's *Goetz* was published in 1799.

In later life Scott realized that 'Matt, though a clever fellow, was a bore of the first description', but he felt indebted to him as the first eminent man of letters to take a serious interest in his work.

36 Archibald Constable (1774–1827)
Andrew Geddes. Oil, 1813.
Scottish National Portrait Gallery

From humble beginnings this 'Prince of Booksellers', as Scott called him, built up the flourishing firm which published the *Edinburgh Review*, the *Encyclopaedia Britannica*, and most of Scott's works. In character he 'was a violent tempered man with those that he dare use freedom with. He was easily overawed by people of consequence, but as usual took it out of those whom poverty made subservient to him. Yet he was generous and far from bad-hearted. In person good looking but very corpulent latterly—a large feeder and deep drinker till his health became weak.' He helped Scott to make a fortune, but the collapse of his firm in the country-wide financial crisis of January 1826 brought about Scott's downfall as well as his own. 'Alas, poor Crafty!' Scott wrote when he died, a broken man. '. . . How he swelled and rolled and reddened, and outblarneyed all blarney. Well, so be it. I hope "After life's fitful fever he sleeps well." '— *Journal* and *Letters*.

37 James Ballantyne (1772–1833) Oil.
Scottish National Portrait Gallery

'J. B.' was for a short time Scott's schoolfellow in Kelso. In 1802 Scott encouraged him to set up his printing-works in Edinburgh and himself became a partner in the firm which printed the Waverley Novels. Scott took more money from the concern than he should have done, and it is fairly clear that it was his fault rather than Ballantyne's that the fall of Constable and Co. involved the ruin of James Ballantyne and Co.

Ballantyne was indispensable to Scott, both as a critic who perfectly represented the popular taste and as the organizer of the system of transcribing and double proofs by which the Author of Waverley's anonymity was preserved. Their close friendship survived the crash, but cooled a few months before Scott's death: he could pardon Ballantyne's addiction to evangelical religion, but not his conversion to Reform.

38 Francis Jeffrey (1773–1850)
Colvin Smith. Oil.
Scottish National Portrait Gallery

A prominent Whig advocate, Jeffrey was editor of the *Edinburgh Review* until 1829 when he was elected Dean of the Faculty of Advocates. In 1830 he became Lord Advocate in the Whig administration. The friendship between Scott and Jeffrey dated from their college days, and survived the political differences of their later years.

39 Lord Melville (1771–1851)
Colvin Smith. Oil.
Scottish National Portrait Gallery

Robert Saunders Dundas, 2nd Viscount Melville, was the son of the great Lord Melville, and First Lord of the Admiralty Scott wrote of him as 'the very early friend with whom I carried my satchel to school'; he was his Colonel in the Yeomanry and an ardent fellow-Tory. Despite a brief estrangement after Scott's *Letters of Malachi Malagrowther*, which criticized the Government of which he was a member, they remained lifelong friends.

40 C. K. Sharpe (1781–1851)
John Irvine. Oil.
Scottish National Portrait Gallery

'Chas Kirkpatrick Sharpe is another very remarkable man. . . . He has infinite wit and a great turn for antiquarian lore. . . . His drawings are the most fanciful and droll imaginable—a mixture between Hogarth and some of those foreign masters who painted temptations of Saint Antony and such grotesque subjects. . . . If he were to make drawing a resource it might raise him a large income. But though a lover of antiquities and therefore of expensive trifles C. K. S. is too aristocratic to use his art to assist his revenue. He is a very complete genealogist and has made many detections in Douglas and other books on pedigree which our nobles would do well to suppress if they had an opportunity. Strange that a man should be curious after Scandal of centuries old. Not but Charles loves it fresh and fresh also . . .'—*Journal*, 20 November 1825.

41 Lord Meadowbank (1777–1861)
Sir Martin Archer Shee. Oil.
Scottish National Portrait Gallery

Alexander Maconochie, elevated to the Bench as Lord Meadowbank in 1819, was not one of Scott's closest friends, although he played a leading role in one important scene in Scott's life. On 23 February 1827, the evening of the Theatrical Fund Dinner, he was asked only as he entered the Assembly Rooms to propose Scott's health. The account of what happened, in Scott's own words to Lady Louisa Stuart, is as follows:

'Ld Meadowbank who is a kind and clever little fellow but somewhat bustling and forward said to me in the drawing room "Do you care any thing about the mystery of the Waverly novels now"— "Not I" I replied "the secret is too generally known"—I was led to think from this that he meant to make some jocular allusion to Rob Roy. . . . But when instead of skirmish of this kind he made a speech in which he seriously identified me with the Author of Waverley I had no opportunity of evasion and was bound either to confess or deny and it struck me while he was speaking it was as good and natural an occasion as I could find for making my avowal. And so out it came to the great astoundishment of all the hearers.'—*Letters*.

42 Sir Robert Peel (1788–1850)
Engraving
Scottish National Portrait Gallery

Scott owed this friendship to the Royal Visit of 1822, when George IV was accompanied by Peel, at that time Home Secretary. They corresponded thereafter, and met whenever Scott was in London. In 1827 Scott confided to his *Journal* the opinion that Peel would be a wise choice as Premier, but the prophecy was not put to the test until 1834, two years after Scott's death.

43 The Duke of Wellington (1769–1852)
Engraving
Scottish National Portrait Gallery

Scott's admiration for the Duke was not far short of idolatry. He once said that not since Julius Caesar had the world seen a great soldier who was also as great a statesman, and he told Ballantyne 'that he had never felt awed or abashed except in the presence of one man—the Duke of Wellington'.

They first met during Scott's visit to Paris in 1815, then in Edinburgh during the Royal Visit of 1822, and thereafter in London and in Northumberland. Wellington assisted Scott in his *Life of Napoleon* by lending his notes on the Russian campaign, and he spoke highly of the work.

44 George Canning (1770–1827)
Engraving.
Scottish National Portrait Gallery

George Canning, 'the witty, the accomplished, the ambitious', first met Scott in 1805, and was associated with him in the founding of the *Quarterly Review*. He became Prime Minister only a few months before his death.

'No man,' Scott wrote of him, 'possessed a gayer and more playful wit in society—

43

THE DUKE OF WELLINGTON.

no one since Pitt's time had more commanding sarcasm in debate. . . . His lash fetched away both skin and flesh and would have penetrated the hide of a rhinoceros.'—*Journal*.

45 Mrs Coutts (1777–1837)
Engraving.
Scottish National Portrait Gallery

Mrs Coutts, formerly the actress Harriet Mellon, was the wife first of Thomas Coutts the banker and after his death of the Duke of St. Albans. She was rich, fat, and vulgar, but Scott found her likeable. When she visited Abbotsford in 1825 it took some puzzling and cramming to accommodate her suite: 'Although she was considerate enough not to come on him with all her retinue, leaving four of the seven carriages with which she travelled at Edinburgh, the appearance of only three coaches, each drawn by four horses, was rather trying for poor Lady Scott.'—Lockhart's *Life*.

THE BLAIR-ADAM CLUB

Each year from 1816 until 1830 Scott spent a June weekend in Kinross-shire with a number of his closest friends. His host was the genial Chief Commissioner of the Jury Court, the Rt Hon. William Adam. Apart from Adam's son and son-in-law, Admiral Sir Charles Adam and Anstruther Thomson, the members of the 'Blair-Adam Club', as it came to be called, were for the most part Scott's intimates from Edinburgh: Adam Ferguson and Will Clerk, Thomas Thomson and his brother the Rev. John Thomson of Duddingston, and from 1818 the Lord Chief Baron of the Exchequer Court, Sir Samuel Shepherd. Thomas Thomson was Vice-President of the Bannatyne Club which Scott had founded in 1823 to publish some of Scotland's older literary and historical works; Clerk and Ferguson had been his close friends since their days at college together, and the Chief Commissioner and Chief Baron were leaders of the legal and social circles in which Scott moved. There was no company in which Scott was happier and no days which he enjoyed more than his annual 'antiquarian skirmish into Fife'.

'We took care to fix it at the period of the longest twilight, and consequently in the season of good weather,' wrote Adam in his privately-printed *Blair-Adam Estate*; 'and we regularly devoted to the *Blair-Adam Antiquarian Club*, at the summer solstice, as much time as we could spare from our duties in Edinburgh. Our arrangement was to dine at Blair-Adam on the Friday, and to remain till the Tuesday morning. By this time we had Saturday and Monday free for our distant expeditions, and for gratifying antiquarian curiosity, in any direction. On Sunday, besides going to the Parish Kirk of Cleish, we could lounge about the grounds.' Adam later told Lockhart that after the Club visited Loch Leven Castle, which Scott described in *The Abbot*, it 'became an object of much increased attention . . . after the author of *Waverley* had, by his inimitable power of delineating character—by his creative poetic fancy in representing scenes of varied interest—and by the splendour of his romantic descriptions, infused a more diversified and a deeper tone of feeling into the history of Queen Mary's captivity and escape'.

Their visit in 1818 was to Castle Campbell, 'when Scott, appearing to possess all the activity of youth, went fearlessly down the yawning gulf into the dungeon'. In subsequent years they went to Dunfermline; Cleish Castle; Macduff's Stone and Abernethy Tower—'where the Author of Waverley dived into the vault, and brought up a human skull, which he wrapped up in a white pocket handerchief, and deposited in the landau'; to St. Andrews and Magus Muir; to St. Monan's Church and Wemyss Castle; to Falkland Palace, which features in *The Fair Maid of Perth*; to Culross, and to Castle Campbell once again.

MEMBERS

46 Sir Walter Scott
Andrew Geddes. Oil, 1818.
Scottish National Portrait Gallery

This portrait of Scott coincides with the commencement of his visits to Blair-Adam. It was painted by Geddes as a study for his large picture of *The Finding of the Regalia of Scotland* (the finished picture now destroyed), and is one of the most sensitive portraits of Scott ever painted.

47 William Adam (1751–1839)
S. W. Reynolds after John Opie.
Mezzotint engraving.
Scottish National Portrait Gallery

The Rt Hon. William Adam of Blair-Adam was a nephew of Robert and James Adam, the architects. He acquired his professional experience at the English bar, and his reputation in the House of Commons, and was Lord Chief Commissioner of the Jury Court throughout its existence from 1816 until 1830.

He was host and presiding genius of the 'Blair-Adam Club', which he entertained each summer. Lockhart calls him 'the only man I ever knew that rivalled Sir Walter Scott in uniform graciousness of *bonhommie* and gentleness of humour'. To Scott he was 'one of the most pleasant, kindhearted, benevolent and pleasing men I have ever known'.—*Journal*.

48 Thomas Thomson (1768–1852)
R. S. Lauder. Oil.
Scottish National Portrait Gallery

Thomson was Deputy Clerk-Register, a brilliant legal antiquarian who brought some order into the records of Scotland, many of which he published for the first time. He edited thirteen works for the Bannatyne Club, of which he was Vice-President and (after Scott's death) President. He was a brother of John Thomson of Duddingston.

47 (detail)   48

49   John Thomson (1778–1840)
R. S. Lauder. Oil.
Royal Scottish Academy

The Rev. John Thomson was minister of Duddingston, but his chief reputation was as a landscape painter. In contrast with the more classically-inspired work of Alexander Nasmyth, under whom he had studied, Thomson's own renderings of coastal scenery shared the same romantic feeling that permeated Scott's work as a novelist.

50   Sir Adam Ferguson (1771–1855)
David C. Gibson. Oil.
Scottish National Portrait Gallery

Adam Ferguson was a schoolfellow of Scott's and the son of Professor Adam Ferguson at whose house Scott met Burns. In 1818, after service in the Peninsula and two years as a prisoner of the French, he became Scott's neighbour at Huntly Burn on the Abbotsford estate.

He married in 1821 the sister of Mrs Jobson, whose daughter Jane married Scott's son Walter a few years later. Through Scott's influence he was appointed Keeper of the Regalia of Scotland, and he was knighted by George IV during the Royal Visit of 1822.

51   Sir Samuel Shepherd (1760–1840)
Colvin Smith. Oil.
Captain C. K. Adam of Blair-Adam

Before coming to Scotland in 1819 as Lord Chief Baron of the Court of Exchequer, Sir Samuel Shepherd had been Attorney-General in London and but for his deafness might have risen higher. 'I like Ch: Ba: Shepherd very much', Scott wrote in his *Journal*, '—as much, I think, as any man I have learned to know of late years.' He was precise, good-humoured and sociable, and much missed when he retired to his native England in 1830.

56

52 Admiral Charles Adam (1780–1853)
Colvin Smith. Oil.
Captain C. K. Adam of Blair-Adam

Charles Adam was the eldest surviving
son of William Adam of Blair-Adam.
Commanding the SYBILLE just before the
Peace of Amiens, he entered a French
port under a hail of red-hot shot from the
batteries and made off with an enemy
frigate. Between 1815 and his promotion
to Rear-Admiral in 1825 he commanded
the Royal Yacht. He represented Kinross
and Clackmannan in Parliament from
1831 to 1841, and was knighted in 1835.

EXPEDITIONS

53 Ravensheugh Castle, Fife
Rev. John Thomson. Oil, 1829.
National Gallery of Scotland

54 St. Andrews, Fife
Rev. John Thomson. Oil.
Mr and Mrs Alan Stark

55 The Firth of Forth
Rev. John Thomson. Oil.
Mr David Edward

56 Fast Castle
Rev. John Thomson. Oil.
National Gallery of Scotland

57 Topographical Drawings
Castle Campbell; Falkland Palace;
Dunfermline Abbey; Inchcolm Priory.
National Gallery of Scotland

58 Abbotsford

A photographic display showing the way
in which Scott drew ideas and models—
and in some cases original fittings—
from the more interesting buildings that
he knew, and brought them to add to the
decoration and interest of Abbotsford.

59 Abbotsford

S. D. Swarbreck. Lithograph.
Dr David Simpson

60 The Abbotsford Family

Sir David Wilkie. Oil, signed, 1817.
Scottish National Portrait Gallery

The painting shows Scott and his family in
peasant dress. From left to right the figures
are Lady Scott, Sophia and Ann Scott, Sir
Walter, a shepherd, Charles Scott, Sir
Adam Ferguson (for whom the picture was
executed), and Walter Scott (later second
baronet).

61 Daniel Terry

William Nicholson. Water-colour.
Scottish National Portrait Gallery

Scott met Terry, the gentleman-actor, in
1810, through the Ballantynes. They were
drawn together by a common taste for
old plays and for the kind of decorations
with which Abbotsford was embellished.
Terry proved a useful agent in London,
buying antiquities and furnishings for the
house. Terry's admiration for Scott knew
no bounds. He looked and frowned and
talked, and even wrote like him.

I T is a kind of Conundrum Castle to be sure and I have great pleasure in it
for while it pleases a fantastic person in the stile and manner of its
architecture and decoration it has all the comforts of a commodious
habitation.'—*Journal*, 7 January 1828.

In 1811, when his lease of Ashestiel was due to expire, Scott bought the
small and unattractive farm-house of Cartleyhole near Melrose from the Rev.
Dr Douglas of Galashiels. It cost him £4,000. The family moved there the
following summer, leaving the neighbours 'much delighted', in Scott's
words, 'with the procession of my furniture, in which old bows, targets, and
lances made a very conspicuous show'. It was on such humble foundations
that there was built the remarkable mansion that was to embody so much of
Scott.

Scott's original plan was to convert the house into a *cottage orné*, with a
conservatory and a fountain, and plans were drawn up by an Edinburgh
architect called Stark. The temptation of buying more land had gripped Scott,
however. In 1813 he acquired the tract between Turnagain and Cauldshiels
Loch; two years later he bought Kaeside; in 1816 Toftfield; in 1817
Huntlyburn, and in 1820 Chiefswood. Inevitably his plans for Abbotsford
were revised and expanded; George Bullock and Edward Blore, the London
architects, were employed to design what we now think of as Scott's
Abbotsford. By 1817 the first large extension was under way, and by January
1823 the roof was on the major part of the building. The house-warming,
which was also a celebration of the engagement of Scott's elder son to Jane
Jobson, was held during the New Year festivities of 1825—almost exactly
a year before Scott's financial ruin.

The interior design was in the hands of William Atkinson, although of
course many of the ideas were Scott's own. The builder was John Smith of
Darnick. Daniel Terry, the actor, assisted considerably in the furnishing of
the house, by acting in effect as Scott's London agent. The total cost was
more than £25,000.

Many of the odd features of Abbotsford had a historical or antiquarian
interest for their owner. A small doorway opening high in the wall came from
the Heart of Midlothian Tolbooth in Edinburgh; the panelling of the entrance
hall is from Dunfermline Abbey; the sundial, with its Greek motto 'For the
night cometh' recalls Dr Johnson's watch; the screen in the garden imitates
part of Melrose Abbey.

Abbotsford still houses Sir Walter's extraordinary collection of treasures.
There are many thousands of books in the library, portraits of members of
the family, the Chantrey bust of Scott himself, and above all a unique
collection of antiquities and curiosities: Napoleon's pistol and gold bee-
clasps, his pen-case and sealing-wax; weapons that belonged to Claverhouse,
Montrose, and Rob Roy; Flora Macdonald's pocketbook, Prince Charlie's
quaich, a fragment of oatcake belonging to a Highlander at Culloden; Rob
Roy's sporran; a tumbler used by Burns; a crucifix belonging to Mary
Queen of Scots; the keys of Loch Leven Castle; medals, medallions and
weapons in profusion. Many of these treasures Scott bought, but many were
presented to him for his collection.

No doubt Abbotsford proved Scott's Delilah, as he himself said. It cost
money that he was able to find only by means of large advances from
Constable, who could afford to accommodate him less easily than everyone
thought. When Constable crashed, and Scott and James Ballantyne went
with him, Scott almost at once thought of the splendid and yet intimate
house which meant so much to him. 'To save Abbotsford I would attempt
all that was possible,' he wrote in his *Journal*. 'My heart clings to the place
I have created. There is scarce a tree on it that does not owe its being to
me, and the pain of leaving it is greater than I can tell.' Happily his creditors
allowed him to continue to live there while he attempted to write off his
debts. When he went abroad in 1831 he left Abbotsford with the greatest
reluctance, and he struggled home to die there within sight of the woods he
had planted and within sound of 'the gentle ripple of the Tweed over its
pebbles'.

59

60

THE ROMANTIC CLIMAX
George IV in Edinburgh

62   Sir Walter Scott

Sir Thomas Lawrence. Oil, 1826.
Graciously lent by Her Majesty The Queen

This painting was commissioned by the King in 1826. Scott noted in his *Journal*: 'Went to sit to Sir T. L. to finish the picture for his majesty which every one says is a very fine one. I think so myself and wonder how Sir Thomas made so much out of an old weather beaten block.'

63   King George IV

Sir Thomas Lawrence. Oil.
Scottish National Portrait Gallery

When he arrived in the Leith Roads with the royal squadron, the King greeted Sir Walter with the words 'The man in Scotland I most wish to see'.

64   The King's Landing at Leith

G. P. Reinagle. Pen and Wash.
Edinburgh Public Libraries

On 15 August, 1822, King George IV landed at Leith: at the spot where he landed a plaque still proclaims 'O Felicem Diem'. Scott himself was not present at the quayside, where the King was received by the Marquess of Lothian, the Lord Clerk Register and the Magistrates of Leith. A procession was formed to bring the King to the city boundary at Picardy Place.

65   The Keys of the City

W. H. Lizars. Engraving.
Dr David Simpson

At a barrier specially erected at Picardy Place, the Lord Provost of Edinburgh presented to the King the keys of the City of Edinburgh. Then the procession, escorted by the Royal Company of Archers, the Royal Scots Greys, the Midlothian Yeomanry Cavalry and the Constables of Edinburgh, moved forward to Holyrood Palace.

ALTHOUGH Sir Walter Scott met the future King George IV for the first time in 1815, he had already exchanged letters with the Prince Regent's court two years earlier when the appointment of Poet Laureate was offered to him. This had caused him some embarrassment because he considered the office (as it then stood) to be a somewhat ridiculous one. In this he was supported by the Duke of Buccleuch, who wrote subscribing to his disapproval and adding 'The poet laureate would stick to you and your productions like a piece of court plaster'.

In March 1815, when the Prince heard that Scott was to be in London, he remarked to J. W. Croker (who has left the record) 'I'll get up a snug little dinner that will suit him'. The meeting at Carlton House, planned in part through William Adam of Blair-Adam, resulted in a friendship between the Prince and the poet that lasted throughout their lives. The two, Croker tells us, 'were the most brilliant story-tellers in their several ways that I have ever happened to meet'. In 1818 it was at the Prince Regent's command that a baronetcy was conferred upon Walter Scott.

Precisely when the idea of stage-managing an entirely novel royal visit to Scotland first occurred to Scott, it is not easy to say. In July 1821 he attended the coronation of George IV in London and wrote an inspired account of the proceedings for the *Edinburgh Weekly Journal*. It was on this occasion too that he sat to Chantrey for the completion of the famous bust. Scott certainly saw the prospective visit not only as an opportunity for the Scottish people to express to the monarch the sentiments of loyalty that he himself felt so deeply, nor to re-enact the Holyrood chapters of *Waverley* with himself and the King playing the principal parts: but above all he saw it as the codification of Scottishness—a moment in time when Celticism and the spirit of the romantic highlander could seek visual expression in a refined statement of the nationality of the Scottish people.

The King landed at Leith on 15 August 1822. Sir Walter had already kissed hands on the ROYAL GEORGE the night before, and on the day itself was deeply concerned that all his arrangements should be right. 'His severest duties,' writes Lockhart 'were those of stage-manager. . . . He had to arrange everything from the ordering of a procession to the cut of a button.' As a result of Scott's plans and of his co-ordination with David Stewart of Garth and the Celtic Society, the two weeks that followed were not only packed with ceremony but were well bedecked with tartan.

Although the King himself stayed at Dalkeith Palace, the home of the Duke of Buccleuch, he held proper court at Holyrood. The keys of the ancient royal palace were duly presented to him, receptions for the ladies and gentlemen of Scotland were held there, and a grand procession was arranged in

'Theme for a Bicentenary', the background music of the exhibition has been specially arranged by Martin J. Ellis, FRCO, and played by him on the organ of Cargilfield Chapel, Edinburgh. It consists of works by nineteenth-century composers who made settings of Scott, and includes: 'Hymne an die Jungfrau'(*Lady of the Lake*)—Schubert; 'Full well our Christian Sires of Old' and 'Where shall the lover rest' (*Marmion*)—Attwood; 'Il était ja-dis un bon roi' (*La jolie Fille de Perth*)—Bizet; 'Ah! verrano' (*Lucia di Lammermoor*)—Donizetti; 'Lied des gefangenen Jägers' (*Lady of the Lake*)—Schubert; 'Oh matutini alboni' (*La Donna del Lago*)—Rossini; and 'Per te d'immensio giubilo' (*Lucia di Lammermoor*)—Donizetti.

66 King George IV at Holyrood
Sir David Wilkie. Oil, 1828.
Scottish National Portrait Gallery

At Holyrood Scott was present to see his
King formally take possession of the
Palace of his ancestors and of the
Honours of Scotland. On his arrival at
Holyrood the King accepted the keys of
the Palace from the Duke of Hamilton
(Hereditary Keeper), with the Duke of
Argyll, in Highland dress, as Keeper of
the Household, and the Duke of Montrose,
as Lord High Chamberlain, in attendance.
He then moved into the building
and received from their traditional
custodians the Honours of Scotland.

67 The Finding of the Honours
Sir David Wilkie. Chalk Drawing.
Scottish National Portrait Gallery

The King, as Prince Regent, had granted
to Scott in 1817 a special warrant to
search in Edinburgh Castle for the

which the King rode to the Castle from the Palace with the Honours of
Scotland borne before him.

From Scott's point of view the royal visit served its purpose, and from the
King's it produced a wide-spread feeling of popular support much needed
at the time. Nevertheless there were critics : the London cartoonists rejoiced
in the King's unwise experiment with Highland dress, and even Lockhart
found a moment to disapprove of 'the kilted rabble'. Cockburn perhaps
spoke for many who held themselves aloof from the fortnight's junketings
when he said 'This glimpse of Royalty did neither good nor harm, and could
not. . . . In giving the people a spectacle at which they gazed exactly as
they would have done at a Chinese Emperor with his gongs, elephants and
mandarins, his visit accomplished all that could be reasonably anticipated.'

At the end of his life the King, who died in 1830, offered two distinctions
to Scott. The first was that of heading the new commission appointed to
examine the Stuart papers at Windsor, and this Scott accepted. The second—
the honour of joining the Privy Council—Scott declined. When he heard
that King George was dead, Scott said, 'He was very kind to me personally,
and a kind sovereign. . . . Much is owing to Kindly recollection of his visit
to this country, which gave all men an interest in him.'

68 (detail)

Scottish Regalia—the Honours of Scotland, comprising sceptre, crown, sword and mace. On 4 February 1818, Scott in company with the Officers of State of Scotland forced open two sealed doors and a great oak chest and recovered from a century of oblivion the proper insignia of the King in Scotland.

68   The Removal of the Honours
Denis Dighton. Oil.
Sir Gregor MacGregor of MacGregor, Baronet

On 12 August 1822, Scott in company with the Knight Marischal of Scotland and escorted by detachments of Clan Gregor and of the Midlothian Yeomanry, duly conveyed the Honours from Edinburgh Castle to Holyrood in preparation for the King's visit.

69   The Procession to the Castle
W. H. Lizars. Engraving.
Dr David Simpson

Probably the grandest moment of the Royal visit in 1822 was the state progress of the King from Holyrood Palace to Edinburgh Castle with the Honours of Scotland borne before him. Alighting at the Castle gates, he derived as much delight as did the assembled crowds from a climb to the ramparts of the Half-Moon Battery: 'Good God!', he remarked, 'What a fine sight: I had no conception that there was such a scene in the world —and to find it in my own dominions!'

70   Highland Dress at the Royal Visit
Sir Gregor MacGregor of MacGregor, Baronet

71   The First Laird in aw Scotia
Anon. Engraving.
Scottish National Portrait Gallery

While Scott and the Celtic Society urged the general adoption of Highland dress on as wide a scale as possible for the Royal Visit, the King's own excursion into the costume of his Scottish ancestors was singularly ill-advised. Not surprisingly it was seized upon with alacrity by the London cartoonists.

72   Sir William Curtis
Anon. Engraving.
Edinburgh Public Libraries

Curtis, Lord Mayor of London, accompanied the King to Scotland and shared with him the adventure into Highland dress. Lockhart wrote: 'In truth, this portentous apparition cast an air of ridicule and caricature over the whole of Sir Walter's Celtified pageantry'.

73   Sir Walter Scott
(After) Sir Francis Chantrey. Marble.
The University of Edinburgh

The Chantrey bust of Scott not only depicts him in the years of his greatest success but also preserves, to quote Lockhart, 'the cast of expression most fondly remembered by all who mingled in his domestic circle'. Chantrey himself describes the circumstances of the first version of the bust (now at Abbotsford): 'My admiration of Scott as a poet and a man induced me in the year 1820 to ask him to sit to me for his bust—the only time I ever recollect having asked a similar favour from anyone. He agreed and I stipulated that he should breakfast with me always before his sittings and never come alone, nor bring more than three friends at once, and that they should all be good talkers.'

Copies of the original bust are to be found in several collections. Chantrey himself records a second version carried out for the Duke of Wellington, while in 1828 he made a third for Sir Robert Peel. In this year he presented his original to Abbotsford.

See cover illustration

SCOTT'S INFLUENCE ABROAD

THE memory of Scott is so closely cultivated in Scotland that he is in danger of being reduced to a tribal hero. In fact he was a citizen of the world. He drew his original inspiration from the Continent. He made the outer world interested, as never before, in Scotland. And his writings were a major force in changing the historical philosophy of Europe.

Scott's first inspiration, in literature, came from German romanticism. In the 1790s he was (in his own phrase) 'German-mad'. He learned German and translated Bürger, Schiller, Goethe. But in him romanticism was always controlled by a sense of history and a rational modern outlook. He soon turned aside from the wilder poets of the *Sturm und Drang* movement and found his permanent German hero in Goethe, 'the Ariosto at once and almost the Voltaire of Germany'. At the height of his fame he received a letter from Goethe. 'Who could have told me thirty years ago', he exclaimed, 'that I should correspond and be on something like an equal footing with the author of *Goetz!*' For the Scottish romanticism of those early years—the unhistorical fantasies of *Ossian* which conquered Europe—the 'Augustan' Scott, the editor of Dryden and Swift, had nothing but contempt.

But in 1815 Ossian disappeared, with Napoleon, from Europe, and a chastened continent demanded a new kind of romanticism: historical, traditional, conservative. In *Waverley* (1814) and its successors, Scott supplied the need. The Scotland which he presented was not vapid, mythological and heroic but a distinct, historic society, ancient and continuous: one of the 'nations' on whose deep-rooted virtues the revolutionary wave had been broken. Europeans were delighted by the spectacle. They even came to see the hitherto unvisited country; for, as a French illustrated guidebook admitted, 'until the publication of *Waverley*, Scotland was hardly known in Europe except in connexion with the revolts of 1715 and 1745'.

The success of the Waverley Novels abroad was indeed phenomenal. They were quickly translated into all major languages. They were read from Moscow to the American frontier and bred everywhere a crowd of imitators. Scott laughed at his imitators, but above the host of 'tushery' novelists stand some great European writers. Balzac and Manzoni, Mickiewicz and Pushkin all confessed and showed his influence. In America he had an imitator in Fenimore Cooper, 'the American Scott', who met Scott in Paris and offered to solve his economic problems by collecting his transatlantic royalties.

The novels were translated into music too, for Scott's heyday was that of the romantic opera, and every librettist was looking for appropriate material. In 1826 the unmusical author sat through an operatic performance of *Ivanhoe* in Paris. *Guy Mannering* and *The Monastery*, conflated into an opera by Boieldieu, had been presented a year earlier; and three years after Scott's death Donizetti produced, in Naples, his masterpiece *Lucia di Lammermoor*. Only Shakespeare provided a richer supply of plots for European opera.

But Scott's greatest influence on the intellectual life of Europe was not immediate, in fiction: it was indirect, through the historical philosophy which underlay his novels and which, by them, he popularised. If any one man made the difference between the historians of the eighteenth and those of the nineteenth century, it was he. For he taught them, instead of looking back on the past, even down on the past, as the unenlightened prelude to the present to look on it direct, respecting its legitimate differences, and illustrating them by sympathetic presentation of its customs, literature, local colour. In so doing, they risked serious error, and their errors ultimately discredited their methods; but at their best they restored to the past its legitimate independence and its vitality.

Almost every great historian of the nineteenth century explicitly admitted the influence of Scott. The French historian of the Norman Conquest, Augustin Thierry, was inspired by *Ivanhoe*. The German Ranke was first carried away by Scott, then rebelled against him, but always retained something of his philosophy. In England, Macaulay rejected his philosophy but adopted his method: his use of local colour and social explanation; while Carlyle saw Scott as the man who had rescued history from dry analysis and restored its humanity. When Carlyle read of Scott's death, he wrote in his Journal, 'he knew what "history" meant: this was his chief intellectual merit'. It was a merit which he taught, with unequal success, to all Europe.

The display which follows illustrates by means of photographs and prints the way in which the expanding influence of Sir Walter Scott impressed itself on the cultural life of Europe.

Scott's devotion to the theatre began, as he tells us in his 'Auto-biography', with the enchantment of *As You Like It*, when he saw it in Bath in his fourth year. He remained a theatre-goer for the rest of his life. His tastes were catholic, and he no doubt overestimated the now-forgotten favourites of the eighteenth century; but he had a fine collection of older plays and a minute acquaintance with all Shakespeare's plays, which reveals itself in innumerable allusions in his novels, letters and journal.

The Theatre Royal, Edinburgh, stood in Shakespeare Square, on the site now occupied by the General Post Office. It opened in 1769, but its heyday was in the time of Scott, who purchased a share in the Theatre and became one of its Trustees in 1809, the year in which Henry Siddons was granted the patent. Siddons was assisted by his wife and brother-in-law, W. H. Murray, and he was responsible for the appearances in Edinburgh of his famous mother and famous uncle, Mrs Siddons and John Kemble. When Siddons died in 1815, Murray became manager in his stead.

Scott had many friends among the actors: Murray and Charles Mackay of the Edinburgh Theatre, Charles Young, Charles Mathews the comedian, John Kemble and Mrs Siddons (both of whom he met at Lord Abercorn's), and above all Daniel Terry. When a fund 'for the relief and support of decayed performers' was set up in 1819, Scott inevitably became one of the patrons, and it was at the Fund dinner in 1827 that he confessed to being the Author of *Waverley*.

His influence on the theatre in Edinburgh, where the puritan distrust of stage plays has never quite been overcome, was immense. According to J. C. Dibdin, the historian of the Edinburgh stage, 'Walter Scott was the person who aroused it from lethargy and stagnation. . . . Scott was above all things a great leader, and in setting the example of regularly patronizing the theatre, he was inevitably followed by the most intelligent of his time.'

His own plays had little success on the stage, but the novels and poems were quickly recognized, both in this country and in France, as the stuff from which popular dramas and melodramas could be manufactured. Playwrights of his own day, and for decades after, concocted version after version of the most popular of them, and almost every novel was the source of at least one play. W. H. Murray, T. J. Dibdin, Isaac Pocock, J. W. Calcraft and Edward Fitzball were the most diligent of the adapters; Daniel Terry had the benefit of Scott's keen interest in all his 'Terryfications' (Scott's own name for them) and his active co-operation in at least one, *Guy Mannering*. This was the first of the long line of adaptations which set a fashion in the whole British theatre.

The Theatre Royal closed for the last time on 25 May 1859 with a programme of comedies, a tableau from *Rob Roy*, and a farewell address from R. H. Wyndham, the lessee:

> Jones, Russell, Mason, Terry, rise to view—
> Terry, the Actor and the Author too,
> Murray, with varied powers, himself a host,
> And he, the Bailie, our peculiar boast:
> While, scattered round, a galaxy of wit,
> Scott, Jeffrey, Wilson, formed the audience fit!—
> O days of byegone glory, tell me when
> We e'er shall look upon your like again?

74 The Theatre Royal
John Leconte. Water-colour.
Edinburgh Public Libraries

75 William Henry Murray (1790–1852)
Sir William Allan. Oil.
Scottish National Portrait Gallery

Murray was associated with the Edinburgh theatre, as actor and manager, for most of his professional life, especially as manager to the Edinburgh Theatre, where he succeeded his brother-in-law Henry Siddons, in 1815. He owed much to Scott, who attended his performances and became a Patron of the Theatrical Fund, which Murray founded in 1819.

76 Charles Mackay as 'Bailie Nicol Jarvie'
Sir William Allan. Oil, 1826.
Mrs Maxwell-Scott of Abbotsford

Charles Mackay was universally known as 'The Bailie' for his inimitable performance of Bailie Nicol Jarvie in *Rob Roy*, acted in the Edinburgh Theatre from 1818 until 1853 — the greatest and most enduring success ever known on the Scottish stage. Scott called his playing of the part 'equal to anything I have ever seen on the stage'. Mackay occasionally called on Scott at Castle Street.

77 The Theatre
A display of playbills of various productions of Scott's novels adapted for the stage.

THE PARLIAMENT HALL

THIS great Hall remains today substantially as it was originally constructed between 1632 and 1642. Many eventful scenes of Scottish history have taken place under its fine oak roof. It was here that the Marquess of Montrose and other leaders debated the Covenanting cause, and it was here only a few years later that Montrose heard the savage sentence of death pronounced on him by his former colleague the Earl of Loudon: many will remember Sir Walter's moving description of the event in *Tales of a Grandfather*. It was in this Hall that the acrimonious debates on the Treaty of Union took place.

After the Union, the Hall became the 'Outer House' of the Court of Session, and three of the judges sat in alcoves on the east side to hear cases which they reported to their colleagues in the adjoining Court (two of the alcoves survive, and are now occupied by statues). In Scott's day the Hall was a hive of activity: the pleaders and their advisers perambulated the floor until a macer called out their case from a window high up in the east wall. Across the end of the Hall was a wooden partition behind which stood a jeweller's and cutler's shop, where Lord Cockburn recalled that he bought his first pair of skates.

The ceiling is of oak from Fife and the Borders, of an almost unique construction to bear the enormous weight of the roof, which has no central support in the middle of the length of the Hall. The large painted-glass south window and the fireplaces are later additions, but the benches round the walls (some of which may date from before the Union) belong to an earlier period. It was in this Hall that Scott trod the floor in his early days, or stood at the fire to talk to his friends, just as the advocates of today walk during Term, discussing their cases or lounging at the same fire.

On the walls are portraits of famous Scottish lawyers (including some by Raeburn, and a small portrait of Scott by Sir David Wilkie). The sculpture is noteworthy, including Roubilliac's statue of Duncan Forbes of Culloden, Lord President, Chantrey's statue of Melville, and the seated statue of Scott by John Greenshields.

The drawings and engravings on display illustrate Parliament House both before and during Scott's lifetime. His friend Skene left a personal record of its appearance and also drew the Musical Festival which was held in these precincts in 1819. Three years later an even more magnificent spectacle took place here when the City of Edinburgh welcomed King George IV at a civic banquet in the Parliament Hall. In 1824 a dramatic fire destroyed much of Parliament Square outside the building, and the reconstruction that followed substantially altered the appearance of a Square that had been a focal point for generations of Edinburgh citizens and businessmen.

THE SCOTT MONUMENT

CERTAINLY the best-known of all public monuments to Scott's memory is the Gothic Tower on Princes Street, Edinburgh. When its foundation stone was laid in 1840, however, two other monuments to Scott had already been erected in Scotland—one in Selkirk and the other in Glasgow. Edinburgh's monument is particularly meaningful in its use of architectural structure and detail copied from Melrose Abbey. In its design the architect, George Kemp, took the buttresses, groined roof, niches and pinnacles from observations he had made at Melrose, and the result embodies the very spirit of romanticism that Scott himself drew from his visits to the Border abbeys.

The design was settled by competition, and the monument was erected at a cost of £15,650, all raised by public subscription. Most of the leading sculptors of nineteenth-century Scotland took a share in providing the profuse figure sculpture. The principal figure of Scott with his dog Maida was modelled by Sir John Steell. Lord Jeffrey composed the inscription laid into the foundation stone :

> This Graven Plate . . . may testify to a distant posterity that his countrymen began on that day to raise an effigy and architectural monument to the memory of Sir Walter Scott Bart., whose admirable writings were then allowed to have given more delight and suggested better feeling to a larger class of readers in every rank of society than those of any author with the exception of Shakespeare alone.

84

83 Scott Monument
Wooden model
Edinburgh City Museums

84 Scott Monument
Portrait of George Meikle Kemp, and photographs from early calotypes by D. O. Hill.
Scottish National Portrait Gallery

NARRATIVE PAINTINGS
AND MEMENTOES

IN the corridor outside the court-room are reproductions of paintings on themes from Scott's novels and poems. His works provided a fruitful source for narrative art throughout the century, and it is possible to show no more than a selection from the vast amount of illustrative painting.

The exhibition here includes many personal possessions of his, which with other memorabilia have been collected from a variety of sources for the exhibition. Scott was himself a collector of such items, and his fame was such that many small objects associated with him have been faithfully preserved.

THIS court room stands as an exhibit in its own right, for it was here that Sir Walter Scott sat below the bench as Principal Clerk of Session. The room is situated in the leg of the L-shaped Parliament House building which was reserved for the Court of Session in the original construction. It was reconstructed and enlarged during Scott's lifetime, but its lay-out remains substantially the same as when the Supreme Court first occupied it in 1639.

It was in this room that Scott set the scene in Chapter 1 of *Redgauntlet*, where Alan Fairford makes his first appearance before the Court as counsel for the absurd and indefatigable Peter Peebles. In the middle of a brilliant argument, Fairford is handed by mistake a letter which tells of the disappearance of his friend Darsie Latimer. 'He stopped short in his harangue—gazed on the paper with a look of surprise and horror—uttered an exclamation, and, flinging down the brief which he had in his hand, hurried out of Court. . . . The Court then arose, and the audience departed, greatly wondering at the talent displayed by Alan Fairford, at his first appearance, in a case so difficult and so complicated. . . . The worst of the whole was, that six agents, who had each come to the separate resolution of thrusting a retaining fee into Alan's hand as he left the Court, shook their heads as they returned the money into their leathern pouches, and said, "that the lad was clever, but they would like to see more of him before they engaged him in the way of business—they did not like his lowping away like a flea in a blanket".'

The Court of Session was founded in 1532 by King James V, father of Mary Queen of Scots. The essential feature of its constitution was that all fifteen of its judges—the 'Haill Fifteen'—sat together to hear argument and to pronounce their decisions. Proceedings before so large a court were far from expeditious, and after the Union in 1707, the Parliament Hall became available for use by the Court and some improvement in the speed of court procedure was achieved by sending individual judges out into the hall to deal with routine business. This arrangement led to the use of the expressions 'Inner House' and 'Outer House', which are still used today. The whole Court sat in the 'Inner House', while the Hall was the 'Outer House'.

Even so, by the beginning of the nineteenth century the delays in litigation had assumed the proportions of a public scandal. The old principle of having the whole Court sitting together was abandoned, and the Court was divided into two Appeal Courts—the First and Second Divisions of the 'Inner House', and Courts of first instance—the 'Outer House'. In addition, a Jury Court was established on an English pattern, and William Adam of Blair-Adam (see no. 47) was brought back from England to organize it.

The Jury Court was subsequently amalgamated with the Court of Session, but the organization of the Court otherwise remains as it was in Scott's lifetime. This court room is occupied by the First Division of the Inner House, an Appeal Court presided over by the Lord President of the Court of Session.

At one time the Court of Exchequer sat in a room above the First Division, on the level of the present gallery in the court room. When the Exchequer Court was abolished, the floor was removed and the gallery constructed. The short-lived Jury Court sat in an adjoining room in Scott's day.

The central feature of the First Division Court is the semi-circular Bench, large enough to accommodate the whole court sitting together, as it does to admit a new judge as a 'Senator of the College of Justice', or very occasionally to hear argument in exceptionally important or difficult cases.

Behind the Bench is the Great Mace of Scotland, which is carried before the Lord President of the Court of Session. It is made of silver gilt, bearing the London hallmark of 1667, and has a striking resemblance to that used by the House of Commons since 1660. The mace emphasizes the fact that the court represents a living link with the days of Scottish independence. During the sittings of the General Assembly of the Church of Scotland, the mace is carried before the Queen's representative, the Lord High Commissioner.

Opposite the bench is the Bar, where advocates stand to plead before the Court. By ancient tradition, the seat of the Dean (the elected leader) of the Faculty of Advocates is in the centre of the Bar.

Between Bench and Bar stands the Clerks' Table, at which Scott sat as Principal Clerk of Session. The Clerk's function was to control the various legal processes being heard each day by the Court, to frame and prepare the orders of the Court for signature by the Lord President, and generally to supervise the arrangement and calling of the cases. The actual chair Scott used, preserved by the Faculty of Advocates, is on display.

Scott's duties were far from onerous, and his *Journal* contains many references to the hours of tedium they involved. Small wonder, therefore, that his fertile imagination should have strayed from the niceties of legal argument to sterner and more romantic incidents. He was drawn by a young advocate 'sitting under the Lords as Clerk of Session, thinking of anything but his business'.

During the exhibition, recorded readings from Scott's works will be played at half-hourly intervals throughout the day. A bell will be sounded in the adjoining rooms just before the start of each reading.

BURKE AND HARE

IN December 1828 people far beyond the boundaries of Edinburgh thrilled to the awful story of the West Port murders. 'Our Irish importation have made a great discovery in Œconomicks', Scott wrote to his daughter in London, 'namely that a wretch who is not worth a farthing while alive becomes a valuable article when knocked on the head and carried to an anatomist and acting on this principle have cleared the streets of some of those miserable offcasts of society whom nobody missed because nobody wished to see them again.'

On Christmas morning, William Burke, a 37-year-old Irishman from Tyrone, was convicted of the murder of Margaret Docherty and condemned to death by hanging. Burke and his landlord Hare (who later turned King's evidence) had sold the corpses of at least sixteen victims to Dr Robert Knox, the anatomist.

Scott did not attend the trial, but was present at Burke's execution on 28 January 1829, a notable public occasion. Along with Charles Kirkpatrick Sharpe he watched from the window of Robert Seton, a bookbinder in the Lawnmarket. 'He died with firmness', Scott wrote to Mrs Hughes, 'though overwhelmed with the hooting, cursing and execrations of an immense mob, which they hardly suspended during the prayer and psalm, which in all other instances in my memory have passed undisturbed.'

This celebrated event in Edinburgh history is commemorated in the passage from the First Division Court to the Parliament Hall by a photographic enlargement of a contemporary engraving.

Up the close and doun the stair
But and ben wi' "Burke and Hare".
Burke's the butcher, Hare's the thief,
Knox the boy that buys the beef.

CASE A
EARLY YEARS

A1 The Ashestiel Manuscript
The manuscript of Scott's fragmentary autobiography, compiled at Ashestiel in 1808 and revised in 1826. The work was not published in Scott's lifetime, but forms the well-known first chapter of Lockhart's biography. A sensitive account of the childhood and education of a man of genius.

A2 Walter Scot, of Satchells
A True History of several Honourable Families of the Right Honourable Name of Scot. Edinburgh, 1688.

Scott's pride in his descent from some of the oldest and boldest Border families showed itself early and never left him. One of the books he first knew and never tired of quoting was the rhyming history of the Scott family compiled at the age of 75 by 'Captain' Walter Scot, a redoubtable soldier of fortune.

A3 Mrs Cockburn
'The most extraordinary genius of a boy.' A letter from Mrs Alison Cockburn (author of *The Flowers of the Forest*, and a kinswoman of Scott's mother) describing the young Scott's prodigious talents, 15 November 1777.

A4 A Collection of Popular Ballads and Tales
Lent by Mrs Maxwell-Scott of Abbotsford

As a small boy Scott indulged his omnivorous appetite for reading and laid the first foundations of his great library by the purchase of chapbooks. This little volume is one of six collections of such chapbooks which he had bound in 1810, and has a note in his hand: 'This little collection of stall tracts and ballads was formed by me when a boy from the baskets of the travelling pedlars. Untill put into its present decent binding it had such charms for the servants that it was repeatedly and with difficulty rescued from their clutches. It contains most of the pieces that were popular about 30 years since and I dare say many that could not now be purchased for any price. W. S. 1810.'

A5 Allan Ramsay
The Tea-table Miscellany. The thirteenth edition. Edinburgh, 1762.

Lent by Mrs Maxwell-Scott of Abbotsford

In the Ashestiel Manuscript, Scott talks of 'two or three old books which lay in the window-seat' at Sandy-Knowe, his grandfather's home near Kelso. From these his Aunt Janet would read to him, and from one, *The Tea-table Miscellany*, he learned by heart the ballad of Hardyknute and declaimed it with such

THIS small selection from an enormous field attempts to show Scott's literary development, from his early ballad collections and verse translations to his own narrative poems, and the transition to the historical novels—the genre for which Scott's talents and temperament so ideally suited him. He brought the historical novel to its highest perfection, and established the pattern which, for better or worse, it held for more than a century after him.

One of the poems, *Marmion*, is shown in manuscript, as are five of the novels—*Waverley, The Heart of Mid-Lothian, The Bride of Lammermoor, The Fortunes of Nigel* and *Redgauntlet*. The others are shown in first editions or the collected editions which appeared in Scott's lifetime. Alongside the poems are a few reminders of the critical reviews, the biographical essays and the editorial projects which would have established his reputation as a man of letters had he never written a novel, or had 'The Author of Waverley' never been identified—the one possibility as unlikely as the other.

As a background to Scott's own works are shown a few of the books which most strongly influenced him. Only a hint can be given of the width and diversity of his reading. He himself said 'My appetite for books was as ample and indiscriminating as it was indefatigable', and the Ashestiel fragment of autobiography tells of his youthful discovery of Scots and English ballads, the plays of Shakespeare, the poetry of Ossian and Spenser, the novels of Richardson, Fielding, Mackenzie and Smollett, and his delight in history of all kinds. Later he learned enough of French, Italian, Spanish and German to enjoy their literatures, and he knew something of Anglo-Saxon and Old Norse, and, of course, Latin. His excellent retentive memory enabled him to call at will on the resources of his reading, and his legal training helped him in his mature years to organize the materials he had gathered.

Scott was one of the most influential writers of the Romantic period, not only in Britain but throughout Europe, where innumerable translations introduced his works to a vast public. His correspondents included the foremost writers of his day—Byron, Fenimore Cooper, Goethe, Washington Irving, Southey and Wordsworth among them. Abbotsford became a place of pilgrimage to the famous and to the obscure, all of whom were received with warm friendliness and hospitality.

Though mainly concerned with Scott the writer, the display tries to give glimpses of the man behind the works—the man of business, the sheriff, the theatre-lover, the Border laird, the sportsman, the genial host and the staunch friend—the friend of hundreds in his lifetime, and through his works and influence, the friend of millions since his death.

Note Publishers are not given in the imprints below. With the exception of the first series of *Tales of My Landlord*, which was published by Blackwood in Edinburgh and Murray in London, the novels shown—from *Waverley* (No. C1) to *Kenilworth* (No. E2)—were published by Constable in Edinburgh with (first) Longman and his partners and (later) Hurst, Robinson & Co. in London. From *St. Ronan's Well* (No. E15) to *The Doom of Devorgoil* (No. H10), Cadell was the Edinburgh publisher. References are given where applicable to William RUFF, 'A Bibliography of the Poetical Works of Sir Walter Scott, 1796–1832' in *Edinburgh Bibliographical Society Transactions*, I (1937–8), and Greville WORTHINGTON, *A Bibliography of the Waverley Novels*, London, 1931.

Unless otherwise stated, books and manuscripts on display are from the collections of the National Library of Scotland.

share in forming my future taste & pursuits I derived from
the old songs and tales which then formed the amusements of
a retired country-family. My grandmother in whose youth
the old border depredations were matter of recent tradition
used to tell me many a tale of Wat of Harden, Wight
Willie of Aikwood, Jamie Tellfer of the fair Dodhead, and
other heroes merrymen all of the persuasion & calling of
Robin Hood & little John. A more recent hero, but not of
less note was the celebrated Deil of Littledean whom whom
She well remembered as he had married her mother's sister.
Of this extraordinary person I learned many a story grave &
gay comic & warlike. Two or three old books which lay on
the window-seat were explored for my amusement in the
lonely winter days. Automathes & Ramsays Teatable miscellany
were my favourites although at a later period an odd volume
of Josephus's wars of the Jews divided my partiality. My
kind & affectionate Aunt Miss Janet Scott whose memory
will ever be dear to me used to read these works to me with
admirable patience until I could repeat long passages
by heart. The ballad of Hardyknute I was early master of
to the great annoyance of almost our only visiter the worthy clergyman
of the parish Dr Duncan who had not patience
to have a sober chat interrupted by my shouting forth this
ditty. Methinks I now see his tall thin emaciated figure,
his legs cased in clasped gambadoes & his face of a
length that would have rivalled the Knight of Lamancha's
& hear him exclaiming "One may as well speak in the mouth
of a cannon as where that child is" with all this acidity
which was natural to him he was a most excellent & benevolent
man, a gentleman in every feeling and altogether different
from those of his order who cringe at the tables of the gentry
or domineer and riot at those of the yeomanry. In
his youth he had been Chaplain in the family of Lord
Marchmont had seen Pope and could talk familiarly of

A15 (detail)

enthusiasm that Dr Duncan, the minister of Smailholm, protested on one of his visits, 'One may as well speak in the mouth of a cannon as where that child is'. Scott's own copy.

A6   Volunteers
Minutes of the Committee of the Royal Edinburgh Volunteer Light Dragoons, 1797–1801.

Scott, one of the instigators of the Company, appears frequently in the minutes as Quartermaster and Secretary, and for a short time Paymaster. 'He was the soul of the Edinburgh troop. . . . It was not a duty with him, or a necessity, or a pastime, but an absolute passion . . .' wrote Lord Cockburn in his *Memorials*.

A7   The Chase, and William and Helen
Two Ballads from the German of Gottfried Augustus Bürger. Edinburgh, 1796. (Ruff 1).

Scott's first literary publication, the fruit of the enthusiasm for the romantic dramas and supernatural ballads of Goethe, Schiller and Bürger aroused by Henry Mackenzie's *Account of the German Theatre*. This copy was given by Scott to his aunt Miss Christian Rutherford.

A8   Goetz of Berlichingen, with the Iron Hand: a tragedy
Translated from the German of Goethe, author of 'The Sorrows of Werter', etc. By William Scott, Esq., Advocate, Edinburgh. London, 1799. (Ruff 3).

The first issue; in the second, the titlepage was cancelled and Scott's name was given correctly. Scott was attracted to Götz primarily by the mediaeval romanticism of the plot. What he gained from translating it was his appreciation of Goethe's use of history and the impetus towards his own creative work.

A9   Thomas Percy,   Bishop of Dromore
Reliques of Ancient English Poetry. 3 vol. London, 1765.

In the Ashestiel fragment, Scott describes his feelings on first reading, during a stay at Kelso about 1783, the work which encouraged him in his own work on Scots ballads. 'But above all, I then first became acquainted with Bishop Percy's *Reliques of Ancient Poetry*. As I had been from infancy devoted to legendary lore of this nature, and only reluctantly withdrew my attention, from the scarcity of materials and the rudeness of those which I possessed, it may be imagined, but cannot be described, with what delight I saw pieces of the same kind which had amused my childhood, and still continued in secret the Delilahs of my imagination, considered as the subject of sober research, grave commentary, and apt illustration.'

A10   Minstrelsy of the Scottish Border
2 vol. Kelso, Printed by James Ballantyne, 1802. (Ruff 11).

Scott's first substantial work as an editor. The first two sections contain old ballads, altered and re-arranged with considerable freedom. The third section consists of imitations by Scott himself and by the friends who shared his interest in the old poetry, notably John Leyden.

A11   James Hogg
'The Ettrick Shepherd'

Letter to Scott of 30 June 1802, in which Hogg (who was to become a close friend) comments on the *Minstrelsy*, 'the first book I ever perused which was written by a person I had seen and conversed with'. He discusses many of the individual pieces, including the authenticity of 'Auld Maitland'.

A12   Thomas the Rhymer
Sir Tristrem; a metrical romance of the thirteenth century. Edited from the Auchinleck MS. by Walter Scott, Esq. Advocate. Edinburgh, 1804. (Ruff 20).

Scott at first intended to include 'Sir Tristrem' in the *Minstrelsy*, but his investigations into the share of Thomas the Rhymer in its composition led him to issue it separately in a text edited from the Auchinleck Manuscript in the Advocates' Library with an introduction and copious notes developing his theory.

A13   The Lay of the Last Minstrel
Lent by His Grace the Duke of Buccleuch

A transcript made from the original manuscript of *The Lay*, with topographical drawings, given by Scott to Lady Dalkeith, 10 January 1805.

A14   The Lay of the Last Minstrel
Graciously lent by Her Majesty The Queen

Scott's own copy of the first edition, with his manuscript notes for the second edition. Presented to Queen Victoria by John A. Ballantyne, 1842. A note by Scott on the flyleaf reads:— 'This copy was prepared for the second Edition upon the principle of abbreviating the notes recommended by the Edinburgh review in their notice of the poem. But my friend Mr Constable would not have the proposed abridgement & so the antiquarian matter was retained. W. S. 15 June, 1821'.

A15   Marmion
The original manuscript, containing many variations from the printed text, open at the well-known description of Edinburgh in Canto IV. According to Lockhart's *Life of Scott*, some of the battle scenes were composed while Scott was galloping his horse along the Portobello sands during the exercises of the Edinburgh Light Dragoons. The handwritten sheets were sent to Ballantyne in batches by post, and were retained at Constable's suggestion. Scott later gave the manuscript (which lacks only a few stanzas) to Archibald Constable; it passed by sale from Thomas Constable to Robert Cadell in 1833, and from Cadell's daughters by another sale to Sir William Augustus Fraser, Bart., who bequeathed it to the Advocates' Library in 1898.

A16   The Life of John Dryden
London, 1808

One of a large paper edition of 50 copies of the *Life* prefixed to Scott's edition of Dryden, published in the same year. When Saintsbury was asked to prepare a new edition of Scott's *Dryden* in 1882, he described it as 'one of the best-edited books on a great scale in English, save in one particular—the revision of the text'. The *Life* is an excellent example of Scott's critical faculty at work on a writer with whose intellect and style he was much in sympathy.

A24

THE

LADY OF THE LAKE;

A POEM.

BY

WALTER SCOTT, Esq.

———————

EDINBURGH:

PRINTED FOR

JOHN BALLANTYNE AND CO. EDINBURGH;

AND

LONGMAN, HURST, REES, AND ORME, AND WILLIAM MILLER,

LONDON;

By James Ballantyne and Co. Edinburgh.

1810.

A17 Wordsworth

A letter from William Wordsworth to Scott, 10 November 1806, in which he comments on Scott's projected edition of Dryden, whose poetic gifts he ranks rather low. The poem transcribed at the end is Wordsworth's 'Glen Almain' (Glen Almond) written on a visit to Scotland.

A18 The Quarterly Review
London, 1815

The *Quarterly* was founded in 1809 as a Tory counter-measure to the Whig *Edinburgh Review*, with Scott as one of the principal promoters and contributors. Among the many perspicacious reviews he wrote for it is that of *Emma* in the number for October 1815. Jane Austen was one of his favourite contemporary writers, and years later an entry in the *Journal* echoed the praise he first voiced in the *Quarterly* : 'That young lady had a

talent for describing the involvements, and feelings, and characters of ordinary life, which is to me the most wonderful I ever met with. The Big Bow-wow strain I can do myself like any now going; but the exquisite touch, which renders ordinary commonplace things and characters interesting, from the truth of the description and the sentiment, is denied to me.'

A19 Jane Austen
Emma. 3 vol. London, 1816.
Lent by Mrs Maxwell-Scott of Abbotsford
Scott's own copy.

A20 The Edinburgh Annual Register
    for 1809 Edinburgh 1811

At about the same time as the *Quarterly* was founded, Scott was helping James Ballantyne to launch the *Edinburgh Annual Register*, which had no comparable

success, though it struggled on for about twenty years. Scott contributed poems and essays on literature and law, and the historical reviews for 1814 and 1815. His anonymous imitation of Crabbe, 'The Poacher', was one of three such imitations, the others being of Thomas Moore and of himself—'The Vision of Triermain', later worked up into *The Bridal of Triermain*.

A21 George Crabbe
Poems. London, 1807

In a letter of 1 June 1813, Scott thanked Crabbe for sending him three volumes of his poems—'now am I doubly armed since I have a set for my cabbin at Abbotsford as well as in town'. This copy belonged to the set he already possessed. Scott admired the strength and sincerity of Crabbe's poems from his first encounter with 'The Village' and 'The Library' in old volumes of Dodsley's *Annual Register* in his uncle's house about 1788, to the days of his last illness, when he asked for Crabbe's poetry to be read to him. They corresponded for many years and Crabbe's visit to Scott in 1822 was a great pleasure to both, though the rival claims of George IV's visit to Edinburgh curtailed their time together.

A22 Byron
English Bards, and Scotch Reviewers. A satire. London, [1809].

In the Romantic movement, Byron's poetry, exotic, passionate and introspective was the antithesis of Scott's vigorous, picturesque narrative—Carlyle's 'Wertherism' as opposed to 'Goetzism'— and it was even more powerful in its impact, here and on the continent. His overwhelming success in the field which Scott had dominated for almost a decade was one of the main causes of Scott's turning novelist. Scott was at first justifiably annoyed by the personal attack on him in *English Bards*, but his reply to Byron's letter of 6 July 1812 treated the matter with such good sense and dignity that the foundations were laid for a close affinity between them.

A23 Byron

A letter of Byron to Scott, 6 July 1812, which opened a friendship between the two men, shortly after John Murray had tried to heal the breach caused by the damaging references in *English Bards*. Byron here reports the Prince Regent's opinion of Scott's poetical works.

A24 The Lady of the Lake, a poem
Edinburgh, 1810. (Ruff 87).
Lent by Dr J. C. Corson

One of twenty copies of the large-paper second impression of the first edition. This copy belonged to Princess Elizabeth, daughter of George III, and has her bookplate. It was probably specially bound for her, in rich red crushed morocco, heavily gilt, with gilt-tooled dentelles and blue shot-silk doublures.

THE

ETTRICKE GARLAND;

BEING

TWO EXCELLENT NEW SONGS

ON

THE LIFTING OF THE BANNER

OF THE

HOUSE OF BUCCLEUCH,

AT THE GREAT FOOT-BALL MATCH ON CARTERHAUGH,

DEC. 4, 1815.

EDINBURGH:

PRINTED BY JAMES BALLANTYNE AND CO.

1815.

A25   Robert Southey

A letter to Scott, 11 May 1810, one of the many Scott received from Southey, in which he praises the newly-published *The Lady of the Lake.*

A26   The Lady of the Lake

The fourth edition. Edinburgh, 1810. (Ruff 91, 108).

This copy has an additional engraved titlepage dated 1811, engravings from illustrations by Richard Westall, and a fore-edge painting of Edinburgh from the Calton Hill.

A27   The Lady of the Lake

Baltimore, 1811. An early American edition. The first edition of *The Lady of the Lake,* which enjoyed considerable popularity in the United States, was published by Edward Earle at Philadelphia in 1810.

A28   Horace Walpole

The Castle of Otranto; a Gothic story. Edinburgh, 1811.

With a note in Scott's handwriting : 'The introduction to this book was written by W. Scott and the frontispiece was drawn by Daniel Terry of Covent Garden Theatre. W. Scott 29th December 1813.' The introduction was used by Scott in 1823, with some alteration, for the memoir prefixed to *The Castle of Otranto* in vol. V of Ballantyne's Novelist's Library.

A29   The Ettricke Garland

Two excellent new songs on the lifting of the banner of the House of Buccleuch, at the great foot-ball match on Carterhaugh, December 4, 1815. Edinburgh, 1815. (Ruff 150).

The first song 'The Lifting of the Banner' is by Scott, the second 'To the Ancient Banner' by Hogg. The match was between the townspeople of Selkirk— the 'Sutors'—and the men of the Vale of Yarrow. The Duke of Buccleuch gave it his patronage, and 'Master Walter Scott, younger of Abbotsford, who attended suitably mounted and armed' displayed the banner of Buccleuch with the ancient war-cry 'Bellendaine' to the crowd of two thousand. Selkirk won the first game after an hour and a half, Yarrow the second after more than three hours. The third was abandoned.

A30   The Field of Waterloo,   a poem
By Walter Scott, Esq. Edinburgh, 1815. (Ruff 147).
Lent by Dr J. C. Corson

The first edition, in original wrappers, uncut. A presentation copy from Scott to his great friend William Erskine, Lord Kinneder, with Erskine's signature on the title-page. The presentation inscription is on the cover.

CASE B
SCOTT & THE LAW

B1 Walter Scott, W.S.
Lent by Dr John Pym
A letter-book containing copies of the outgoing professional correspondence of Sir Walter Scott's father, October 1778–August 1779. Amongst his clients was Stuart of Invernahyle, 'who had been out in both 1715 and 1745, and whose tales were the absolute delight of my childhood', as Scott remarked in a letter of 1806. Scott valued his apprenticeship to his father, which grounded him thoroughly in legal practice, but later 'prayed devoutly' that he would not need to plague himself with 'rent rolls, annuity tables, purchase and redemption of leases, and all the endless train of complicated chicanery' of an attorney's business.

B2 Disputatio Juridica,
Ad Tit. XXIV Lib. XLVIII Pand.
De Cadaveribus Damnatorum quam . . . pro advocati munere consequendo, publicae disquisitioni subjicit Gualteris Scott, Auct. et Resp. Ad diem 10 Julii, hor. loc. sel. Edinburgi, apud Balfour et Smellie, Facultatis Juridicae Typographos. M,DCC,XCII.
Scott's Latin thesis discussing the disposal of the dead bodies of condemned criminals, which formed the subject of his public trial on admission to the Faculty of Advocates. The work is dedicated to the notorious Lord Braxfield.

B3 Admission to the Bar
After giving up his training as an apprenticed Writer to the Signet, Scott turned to work for admission to the Faculty of Advocates. This document shows his formal application to the Court of Session for admission to the Bar examinations, referred by the Lord President to the Faculty, and by the Dean of Faculty to his examiners. Subsequent pages record the various trials, a process well described in *Redgauntlet*. This document has recently been cited in support of an argument that Scott was born in 1770, but other evidence demonstrates clearly that 1771 is correct. Scott was therefore admitted to his Bar examinations slightly before the statutory age.

B4 Speculative Society Minutes
Lent by the Society
Scott was a keen member of the Speculative Society, a small Edinburgh literary and debating club which survives to this day, with premises in the Old College of the University. He was elected in 1790, and became Secretary a year later. The minutes for several years are in his hand, and the volume is open at the record of a debate led by Scott on 19 March 1793.

B5 Mark Napier Sketch
A sketch of Scott at the Clerks' table, made in a copy of Welsh's *Life of Professor Thomas Brown*. The artist, Mark Napier, provides the inscription: 'Sir Walter Scott as he was, 1829, sitting under the Lords as Clerk of Session, thinking of anything but his business. M.N.'

B6 Caricature
Lent by George Scott-Moncrieff, Esq.
Another Parliament House sketch of Sir Walter Scott, made by Robert Scott Moncrieff of Fossaway, Advocate, between 1816 and 1820.

B7 Advocates' Library
Scott took a lively interest in the affairs of the Advocates' Library, founded in 1682 by Sir George Mackenzie of Rosehaugh, and he was a Curator for many years. One of his borrowing-slips, for a volume of Defoe taken out in 1810, is displayed. The Library became the National Library of Scotland in 1925, when the Faculty transferred all but their legal books and manuscripts to the nation. The collection of law books is maintained as the working library of the Scottish Bar.

B8 Resignation
Scott's letter of 6 November 1830 in which he submits his formal resignation from the Clerkship to Charles Hope, Lord Granton, Lord President of the Court of Session.

CASE C
THE NOVELS I

The Library has drawn on the riches of its Hugh Sharp Collection to show first editions of all the novels from *Waverley* to *Ivanhoe* (with the exception of *The Bride of Lammermoor* and *A Legend of Montrose*)—all exceptionally fine copies in the original boards. For the later novels examples are shown of collected editions and foreign editions published in Scott's lifetime.

C1 Waverley
The original manuscript of the novel published in 1814.

As is well known from Scott's General Preface to the 'Magnum Opus' edition, the novel had been started some years earlier, but the manuscript was laid aside. It was rediscovered by accident when Scott was searching for fishing-tackle in a drawer at Abbotsford. This chance led him to finish the story, which was accomplished at great speed.

Waverley was not set up from this manuscript: an intermediate copy was made by Ballantyne so that the printers would not recognize the writing, and anonymity was preserved. The holograph has the characteristic appearance of all Scott's prose manuscripts. It is written fluently and compactly (both habits probably acquired when Scott was apprenticed to his father), with revisions, on the facing pages.

The manuscript was presented by Scott to Constable in 1823. It was sold at auction for only £18 in 1831, and was presented to the Faculty of Advocates in 1850. A further small portion of the text (this MS. is not complete) is in the Pierpont Morgan Library.

C2 Waverley
Or, 'Tis Sixty Years Since. 3 vol. Edinburgh, 1814. (Worthington 1).

The first edition, from the Hugh Sharp Collection. This copy was originally bought for a Book Club and the fly-leaf of volume 2 has a manuscript list of the subscribers.

C3 Waverley
A letter from Scott to his friend John Bacon Sawrey Morritt, 9 July 1814, in which he refers to 'a small anonymous sort of a novel in 3 volumes', newly published. 'It has made a very strong impression here and the good people of Edinburgh are busied in tracing the author and in finding out originals for the portraits it contains.' Morritt was one of the few to be let in to the secret of the author's identity.

C4 Guy Mannering or, The Astrologer.
By the Author of 'Waverley'. 3 vol.
Edinburgh, 1815. (Worthington 2).

The first edition, from the Hugh Sharp
Collection.

C5 Daniel Terry
Guy Mannering; or, the gipsey's prophecy:
a musical play. London, 1816.

The first, and one of the best, of the long
succession of plays based on the Waverley
Novels. The adaptation was by Daniel
Terry, actor and theatre-manager, a close
friend of Scott's. Scott, always a theatre-
lover, took a keen interest in this and
subsequent 'Terryfications'.

C6 Alexander Campbell
Albyn's Anthology, or, A select collection
of the melodies and vocal poetry
peculiar to Scotland and the Isles.
2 vol. Edinburgh, 1816.

Alexander Campbell (1764–1824),
musician and writer, was Scott's music
tutor. In later years Scott supported
Campbell in his project of collecting Scots
melodies and supplied some of the poetry
for them. A slight threat to the anonymity
of 'the author of *Waverley*' arose when he
gave the 'Lullaby of an Infant Chief' to
Campbell for *Albyn's Anthology* and to
Terry for the play of *Guy Mannering* at
almost the same time, but Scott solved it to
his satisfaction by getting Campbell to
include the verses anonymously, and
trusting that, since they were set to different
music, the link between anthology, play
and novel would pass unnoticed.

C7 The Antiquary
By the Author of 'Waverley' and 'Guy
Mannering'. 3 vol. Edinburgh, 1816.
(Worthington 3).

The first edition, from the Hugh Sharp
Collection.

C8 Tales of my Landlord [First Series]
Collected and arranged by Jedediah
Cleishbotham, schoolmaster and parish-
clerk of Gandercleugh. (The Black
Dwarf and Old Mortality.) 4 vol.
Edinburgh, 1816. (Worthington 4).
The first edition, from the Hugh Sharp
Collection.

C9 John Galt
Ringan Gilhaize; or the Covenanters.
3 vol. Edinburgh, 1823.

Galt's great merit as a novelist was his
ability to give an authentic picture of
ordinary life in contemporary Scotland,
as he did in *Annals of the Parish* and *The
Entail*. When he challenged Scott in
historical fiction and set out, in *Ringan
Gilhaize*, to show the Covenanters in a
more favourable light than Scott had done
in *Old Mortality*, he fell far short of
Scott's skill in the integrated and
imaginative use of his sources, and the
variety and depth of his character-drawing.
Nevertheless his insight into the motives
of the Covenanters and sympathy for their
sufferings make his novel a useful com-
panion-piece to Scott's far greater work.

C4

GUY MANNERING;

OR,

THE ASTROLOGER.

BY THE AUTHOR OF " WAVERLEY."

'Tis said that words and signs have power
O'er sprites in planetary hour;
But scarce I praise their venturous part,
Who tamper with such dangerous art.
Lay of the Last Minstrel.

IN THREE VOLUMES.

VOL. I.

EDINBURGH:
Printed by James Ballantyne and Co.
FOR LONGMAN, HURST, REES, ORME, AND BROWN,
LONDON; AND ARCHIBALD CONSTABLE AND CO.
EDINBURGH.

1815.

C10 Rob Roy
By the Author of 'Waverley', 'Guy
Mannering', and 'The Antiquary'. 3 vol.
Edinburgh, 1818. (Worthington 5).
The first edition, from Hugh Sharp
Collection.

C11 Isaac Pocock
Rob Roy Macgregor or, Auld lang
syne. An opera. London, 1820.

By far the most popular and longest-lived
of all the Waverley Plays. Pocock's
version, with music arranged by John
Davy, was the most satisfactory of
several adaptations. It was produced at
Covent Garden in March 1818, and played
all over Great Britain and America
during the nineteenth century and, in
Scotland, well into the twentieth.

C12 Playbill

For the Drury Lane production of *Rob Roy the Gregarach*.

An adaptation—almost a travesty—by George Soane, in which Helen Macgregor becomes Rob Roy's mother, Francis Osbaldistone disappears, and Rob Roy and Diana Vernon become a pallid pair of young lovers. It was rushed on in March 1818 to compete with Pocock's version but it was badly received and lasted only a few nights.

C13 The Heart of Mid-Lothian

The original manuscript of *The Heart of Mid-Lothian*, published in June 1818 only six months after the appearance of *Rob Roy*. The page shown, with the verses of 'Proud Maisie', indicates Scott's facility in the composition of the poems, apparently written straight on to the page.

C14 Tales of my Landlord

Second series, collected and arranged by Jedediah Cleishbotham, Schoolmaster and Parish-Clerk of Gandercleugh. (The Heart of Mid-Lothian.) 4 vol. Edinburgh, 1818. (Worthington 6). The first edition, from the Hugh Sharp Collection.

C15 The Bride of Lammermoor
The original manuscript.

Lent by the Signet Library

This manuscript contains the bulk of the novel, but some portions of it are missing, and others (which have not survived) were dictated to William Laidlaw when Scott was ill in 1819.

C16 The Bride of Lammermoor

The displayed portion of this page-proof shows the printer's exasperation with the copy sent for the opening of chapter V. Scott made numerous revisions after his books had been set up in type, and his proof-sheets are important for showing the transmission of the text.

C17 Ivanhoe, a romance

By the Author of 'Waverley', etc. 3 vol. Edinburgh, 1820. (Worthington 8).

The first edition, from the Hugh Sharp Collection.

The Management, zealous in every thing that can contribute to public accommodation, has availed itself of the short Easter recess in warming and ventilating the Interior ;—in lighting the House by a new and splendid CHANDALIER ; and in beautifying and decorating the SALOON.

The STOVES which have been constructed, upon a new principle, exclude the cold and raw Air, and introduce into the body of the House a mild and refreshing temperature ; while the active and powerful Ventilator draws off the damps, and renders salubrious the auditory part of the Theatre.

The new brilliant CHANDALIER, lighted by Gas, is an improvement upon every thing that has hitherto appeared,—it sheds a clear, soft, and beaming Light over the House, neither obstructing the sight, or diminishing the interest of the Stage.

The SALOON has undergone a thorough and complete change, and will be opened as usual, for the accommodation of the Half-price Company.

THEATRE ROYAL, DRURY-LANE.

This Evening, Saturday March 28, 1818.

Their Majesties' Servants will perform (for the 4th time) a New Romantick Drama, in Three Acts, called

ROB ROY,
The GREGARACH.

The Story partly original, and partly founded on the popular Romance of ROB ROY.
With New SCENERY, MACHINERY, DRESSES and DECORATIONS.

The Overture composed and selected, and the incidental Musick composed by Mr. T. COOKE. The Scenery designed by Mr. GREENWOOD, and painted by him and Assistants. The Machinery by Mr. LETHBRIDGE, and the Decorations executed under his direction, by Messrs. Murphy, Sutton, Kelly, and Assistants.—The Dresses by Mr. BANKS, and Miss SMITH.—Decoratrice, Miss ROBINSON.

General Vernon, Mr. B E N G O U G H,
Sir Rashleigh Osbaldistone, Mr. R A E,
Rob Roy Macgregor *(Chief of the Clan Gregaraich)* Mr. H. J O H N S T O N,
Captain Edwards, Mr. B A R N A R D,
English Officer, Mr. F I S H E R, English Serjeant, Mr. K E N T,
Morvyn, *(a Seer)* Mr. H O L L A N D,
Mac Malloch, *(an Ancient Bard)* Mr. R. P H I L L I P S,
Dougal, } Mr. W A L L A C K,
Allan, } Highlanders of the Clan Macgregor Mr. S M I T H,
Hamish, } Mr. W O O L F,
Murdoch, Mr. J. S M I T H,
Allister, Mr. C O V E N E Y,
Andrew Hollywood, Mr. K N I G H T.
Diana Vernon, Miss S M I T H S O N,
Ellen Macgregor, *(Mother of Rob Roy)* Mrs. G L O V E R,
Rose, Mrs. B L A N D,
Elspeth, Miss C U B I T T, Janet, Mrs. B E L L C H A M B E R S.

Scotch Peasants and Highlanders.—Messrs. Clarke, Caulfield, Cook, Jones, Dibble, Saunders, Hope, G. Wells, Goodman, Mathews, Vials, Cooper, Brown, Oddwell, Mead, Wilson, Evans. Mesdms. M. Cooke, Caulfield, Cause, Lyon, Corri, Vials, Goodman, Taylor, Calvert, Ivers, Carr.

The Prologue to be Spoken by Mrs. KNIGHT,
The Epilogue by Mr. WALLACK and Mr. KNIGHT.
To which will be added, the Farce of

WHAT NEXT!

Colonel Touchwood, Mr. DOWTON, Major Touchwood, Mr. HARLEY,
Mordaunt, Mr. KENT, Colonel Clifford, Mr. BARNARD,
Sharp, Mr. KNIGHT, Brief, Mr. HUGHES, Snaggs, Mr. OXBERRY,
Prudence, Mrs. HARLOWE, Clarissa, Mrs. ORGER, Sophia, Miss IVERS.

Vivant Rex et Regina. *No Money to be returned.* *Rodwell, Printer, Theatre Royal, Drury.*

The New Romantick Drama of

ROB ROY, the Gregarach,

On its third representation last Night, was honoured with added success, having again obtained from a brilliant Audience the most enthusiastick and continued bursts of Approbation throughout, both to the striking interest of the Piece, and the picturesque beauty of the Scenery, it will therefore be repeated every Evening till further Notice.

Mr. MUNDEN having unfortunately experienced some relapse, the COBBLER of PRESTON, intended for representation this Evening, must necessarily be postponed.

On Monday, The Farce of HONEST THIEVES.
On Tuesday, A favourite ENTERTAINMENT.
On Wednesday, will be produced, for the first time, a New FARCE, called

The SLEEPING DRAUGHT,

Principal Characters by Mr. Hughes, Mr. Gattie, Mr. Barnard, Mr. Harley, Mr. Knight, Mr. Ebsworth, Mr. Coveney, Mr. Minton, Miss Ivers, Mrs Hughes.

** Various other NOVELTIES are in active preparation.

C18

The following Lines, are written by Sir Walter Scott Bart.— The first Verse is a literal translation of a GERMAN MOTTO, engraved round a Dish of curious Workmanship, containing a little Figure, holding on his head, a small Tray with a bit of Silver Ore in it, and several other Minerals scattered in the dish which is of Copper richly gilt.
The two other Verses are in compliment to LORD GRAY's Family.

My Mither is of sturdy airn,
A copper Dwarf am I, her Bairn;
Of Silver ore, a tray I hold,
And am clad o'er with beaten gold.

The airn speaks stalworth heart and hand,
The copper wealth and wide command,
The Silver rank and noble name,
The gold true worth and spotless fame.

Long have they flourish'd, long may they,
Still flourish in the House of GRAY.

Printed at KINFAUNS CASTLE, Novr. 19th. 1823.

C18 Félicité Lagarenne
Costumes d'Ivanhoe au Bal donné par LL. AA. R. et I. le Prince et la Princesse d'Orange à Bruxelles le 5 fevrier, 1823. [Brussels, 1823.]
A sidelight on Ivanhoe's immense popularity on the Continent.

C19 My Mither is of Sturdy Airn
Printed at Kinfauns Castle, Novr. 19th, 1823. (Ruff 159).
The only copy known. Kinfauns Castle was the Gothic mansion near Perth built for Francis, 14th Lord Gray, in 1822. The catalogues of the books and pictures he collected there are the only other known productions of this press. An earlier edition of this poem has the imprint 'Printed at Gray House [the earlier family seat] Sept. 1st 1818', and the only known copy is in Edinburgh University Library. Nothing is known of the circumstances in which the poem was written.

CASE D
THE STAGE

D1 Joanna Baillie
The Family Legend: a tragedy. Edinburgh, 1810.

Joanna Baillie was a friend and correspondent of Sir Walter from their first meeting in London, where she lived for most of her life, though a Scot by birth and upbringing. When *The Family Legend* was produced at the Theatre Royal in Edinburgh in January 1810, Scott wrote the prologue, supervised the production, and wrote enthusiastically to Miss Baillie of its 'complete and decided triumph'.

D2 Joanna Baillie

A characteristic letter from Joanna Baillie, 21 October 1809, referring to her play *The Family Legend*, which she submitted for Scott's opinion. She writes of possible economies which might be made in the event of it being accepted for production by Henry Siddons.

D3 Daniel Terry
The Antiquary: a musical play, in three acts; taken from the celebrated novel of that name, and first produced at the Theatre Royal, Covent Garden, on Tuesday, 25 January 1820. London, 1820.

Terry revised the first unsuccessful stage version made by Isaac Pocock for Covent Garden in 1818. His 1820 version had greater success, thanks largely to the spectacular stage effects in the scene of the cliff rescue, shown in this prompt copy.

D4 The Heart of Mid-Lothian
A romantic national drama, as performed at the Theatre-Royal, Edinburgh. Edinburgh, [1823].

Dibdin's version, with modifications. *The Heart of Mid-Lothian* lent itself well to dramatic treatment and became one of the most popular of the novels on the stage. The version by Thomas J. Dibdin, actor, manager and prolific playwright, was the first of many adaptations. It was produced in London in January 1819 and was used, with considerable changes, probably by J. W. Calcraft, for W. H. Murray's production at the Theatre Royal in Edinburgh in February 1820.

D5 The Heart of Mid-Lothian
Playbill for the performance 'fourth time in this city' at the Theatre Royal, Edinburgh, 26 February 1820.

D6 Alexander Nasmyth
Designs for *The Heart of Mid-Lothian*. Lent by the National Gallery of Scotland

Executed for the production at the Theatre Royal, Edinburgh in 1820. The drawings show the ruins of St. Anthony's Chapel, the Grassmarket, the Parliament Close, and three prospects of the City.

D7 Edward Fitzball

Waverly; or sixty years since: a dramatic romance, in three acts. At first performed on Monday, 8 March 1824, at the Adelphi Theatre, Strand, London.

Waverley was comparatively late in coming to the stage and never achieved great popularity. Such success as Fitzball's version had was largely due to the performance of Mrs Waylett in the singing role of Davie Gellatley.

D8 John William Calcraft

The Bride of Lammermoor. A drama; in five acts. Edinburgh, 1823.

Calcraft was the stage name of J. W. Cole, a member of Murray's company from 1819 to 1824, subsequently manager of the Theatre Royal, Dublin, and Charles Kean's secretary and biographer. He adapted at least five of the Waverley Novels for the stage. Dibdin forestalled him with a version of *The Bride of Lammermoor* in London in 1819, but Calcraft's met with much greater success and was often revived in Edinburgh, London, Dublin, and in America.

D9 Redgauntlet, a drama

Founded on the tale of the same name by the author of 'Waverley'. Edinburgh, 1824.

The adaptation was probably by W. H. Murray, brother of Harriet Siddons and manager of the Theatre Royal from 1815 to 1848. He gave it for the first time for his benefit on 28 May 1825, but it had only three performances at the time and never became popular.

D10 Auber

Leicester, ou Le Chateau de Kenilworth. Opéra comique. Paroles de MMrs. Scribe et Melesville. Musique de D. F. E. Auber. Paris, [1823].

The popularity of *Kenilworth* as a source for playwrights and librettists is rivalled only by *Ivanhoe* and *The Bride of Lammermoor*. They were particularly popular in France where the melodramatists revelled in their disguises and duels, murders and madness. Auber's opera was produced at the Opéra Comique in January 1823 and played there more than sixty times in the next five years.

D11 Donizetti

Lucia di Lammermoor. Tragedia lirica in due parti. Poesia del Signer Salvatore Cammarane. Musica del Signor Maestro Cav. Gaetano Donizetti. [The libretto.] Napoli, 1840.

The best and best-known of the operas based on Scott's works, first produced in Italy in 1835 and still frequently performed.

REDGAUNTLET

A DRAMA;

FOUNDED ON THE TALE OF THE SAME NAME

BY THE

AUTHOR OF WAVERLEY

&c. &c.

PUBLISHED BY

JOHN ANDERSON JUNr 55.NORTH BRIDGE STREET

EDINBURGH.

1824.

D12 Schubert

Sieben Gesänge aus Walter Scott's Fräulein vom See. Op.52. Hft.1. Wien, [1834].

Scott maintained that he was usually unsuccessful in composing words to a tune 'although my friend Dr. Clarke and other musical composers have sometimes been able to make a happy union between their music and my poetry'. Schubert is the most eminent of the many composers who have effected this union. His settings for seven songs from *The Lady of the Lake* were composed in 1825 and first published in 1826. The German words were from the translation of the poem by Adam Storck published in 1819. Scott had a copy of the translation sent to him by Storck, but he never refers to Schubert's settings.

D13 Rossini

La Donna del Lago. Paris, [1824].

Scott's poems, even before his novels, were treasure trove for playwrights in search of plots. There were several versions of *The Lady of the Lake* before Rossini's opera, with a libretto by Andrea Leone Tottola, was produced at Naples in 1819 and London in 1823.

D14 Boieldieu

La Dame Blanche, opéra-comique. Musique de M. Boyeldieu. (In Oeuvres complètes de M. Eugène Scribe, tom.10. Paris, 1841).

Scribe drew on *Guy Mannering* and *The Monastery* to concoct a libretto which fitted so happily with Boieldieu's delightful music that the opera was an instantaneous success on its production in Paris in December 1825, maintained its popularity through the nineteenth century and has been occasionally revived in the twentieth.

CASE E
THE NOVELS II

E1 Lives of the Novelists
2 vol. Paris, 1825.

Anne Scott's copy. Written as prefaces to Ballantyne's Novelist's Library, one of John Ballantyne's publishing ventures begun in 1821. They were issued separately by Galignani in two volumes in 1825 and in the following year Scott wrote to Lady Louisa Stuart,—'I am delighted they afford any entertainment for they are rather flimsily written being done merely to oblige a friend. They were yoked to a great illconditioned lubberly double-columned book which they were as unfit to tug along as a set of fleas would be to draw a mail-coach.'

E2 Kenilworth
Historical Romances of the author of Waverley. Vol. VI. Edinburgh, 1822.

A volume of the first collected edition. The separate publication of the novels was followed by publication in sets, with new sets and new editions of existing sets being added as the novels mounted up: Novels and Tales, 1819; Historical Romances, 1822; Novels and Romances, 1824; Tales and Romances, 1827–33.

E3 The Pirate
Or The Sisters of Burgh Westra; a tale of the islands of Shetland and Orkney. Epitomized from the celebrated novel of the same title, written by the Author of Waverley, by Sarah Scudgell Wilkinson. London, 1822.

At least fifteen of the Waverley novels appeared as chapbooks during Scott's lifetime, some in several different versions. Most were anonymous, but Sarah Scudgell Wilkinson condensed *Waverley, Kenilworth,* and *The Fortunes of Nigel,* as well as *The Pirate.* They cost anything from a penny to sixpence and gave the young and the poor a far-off glimpse of what those who could afford it bought for a pound or two.

E4 Olaus Magnus
Historia de gentibus septentrionalibus. Romae, MDLV.

The edition to which Scott specifically refers in *The Pirate,*—'the fine edition published in 1555 which contains representations of the war-chariots, fishing exploits, warlike exercises, and domestic employments of the Scandinavians, executed on copper-plates.' Scandinavian influence appears directly in *The Pirate,* but in many of his other works Scott reveals his acquaintance with the literature, mythology and customs of the northern nations.

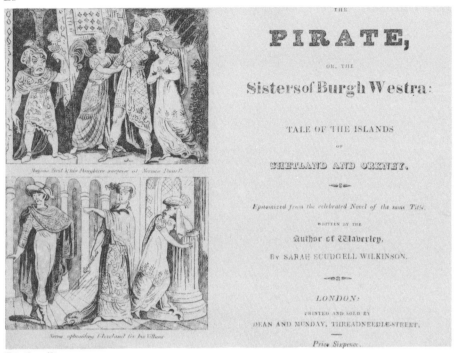

E3

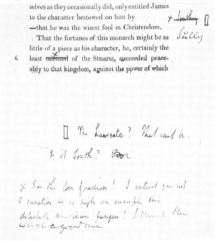

E8 (detail)

E5 James Fenimore Cooper
The Pilot, a tale of the sea. 3 vol. London, 1824.
Lent by Mrs Maxwell-Scott of Abbotsford

The Pilot was the direct result of *The Pirate.* Cooper, who knew life at sea from personal experience, wrote it to demonstrate that he could replace Scott's 'vraisemblance' by accuracy of nautical detail that would satisfy even the experts. His early novels of adventure and romance set against an American background gained for him the label of 'the American Scott' (not at all to his liking); but it is by the social analysis and criticism of his later novels that he holds his place in American literature.

E6 Fenimore Cooper
A letter from J. Fenimore Cooper to Sir Walter Scott, 12 September 1827, on the copyright problems of an American edition of Scott's works.

E7 The Fortunes of Nigel
The original manuscript.
Lent by King's School, Canterbury

This volume was owned in the nineteenth century by John Ruskin—a learned and enthusiastic admirer of Scott—and subsequently by another enthusiast, Sir Hugh Walpole, who left it to his old school.

Walpole bequeathed to the National Library his set of Sir Walter Scott's private letterbooks, which joined the Abbotsford manuscripts and thus reunited Scott's incoming correspondence.

E8 The Fortunes of Nigel
Corrected proofs, with annotations by Scott and James Ballantyne. The page shown (127) contains Ballantyne's objection to 'talented' (of which this is, surprisingly, an early example) as an Americanism.

E9 Thomas Shadwell
The Squire of Alsatia. London, 1688.

Shadwell's *Squire of Alsatia* provided much of the background and thieves' cant for Nigel's sojourn in Whitefriars. Scott knew the early English dramatists well, as the chapter-headings of the novels show—even allowing for his confessed practice of supplying lines from imaginary 'Old Plays' when his memory produced no appropriate quotation.

E10 Carle, Now the King's Come
A proof copy, with corrections, in Scott's hand, of his lines on George IV's visit to Scotland in 1822.

E11 King's Visit

The original manuscript of Southey's 'Ode written after the King's Visit to Scotland, 1822', one of the many poetical commemorations of the event.

E12 Crabbe

Lines. On the King's visit. [Edinburgh, 1822.]

Even Crabbe, the least likely of royal panegyrists, succumbed to the prevailing mood during his visit to Scott in August 1822.

E13 King's Visit

A letter to Scott from William Henry Murray, the actor and manager of the Theatre Royal, 1822. He writes that his theatre's loss will be severe if the King chooses to see a performance with Edmund Kean, who was playing a starring engagement at the Theatre Royal while the King was in Edinburgh: '. . . I once more solicit your influence that his Majesty may be induced to command one of the National plays, which will release us from our very awkard situation.' The King obediently commanded *Rob Roy*, and it was played on 27 August with Mackay in his most famous part as the Bailie and Harriet Siddons as Diana Vernon, to the great satisfaction of the King, the company, and the intolerably crowded audience, but to the deep chagrin of Kean.

E14 Quentin Durward

By the author of 'Waverley', 'Peveril of the Peak', etc. 3 vol. Paris, 1823.

A French edition of the novel which had a special appeal for French readers and encouraged Scott's French followers in the exploration of their own history.

E15 St. Ronan's Well

Tales and Romances of the Author of Waverley, vol. I-II. Edinburgh, 1827.

A volume of the first collected edition in the duodecimo format issued almost simultaneously with the larger octavo volumes.

E16 Redgauntlet

The original manuscript.

The page exhibited contains part of 'Wandering Willie's Tale'. The well-known portrait of Sir George Mackenzie —'the Bluidy Advocate Mackenzie, who for his worldly wit and wisdom had been to the rest as a god'—was added in proof, and does not appear in the manuscript.

E17 Redgauntlet

A tale of the eighteenth century. By the author of 'Waverley'. 2 vol. Philadelphia, 1824.

The novels were immensely popular in the United States and various publishers rushed them into print in America as soon as they could get hold of British copies. Carey of Philadelphia outstripped his rivals by planting what we should now call an industrial spy in Ballantyne's printing works and printing his edition from purloined advance sheets. This has provided important bibliographical information about Scott's revision of his texts.

E18 Woodstock

Waverley Novels. vol. XXXIX. Edinburgh, 1832.

A volume of the 'Magnum Opus', the complete edition of the Waverley Novels with Scott's final revisions, new introductions and additional notes, published in 48 volumes between 1829 and 1833. He worked on it during the last years of his life in the hope that it would play a major part in paying off the debts he incurred after the failure of Ballantyne and Constable—as indeed it did.

CASE F
ABBOTSFORD

F1 Lady Scott

Sir Walter's home-life was happily founded on his marriage. In 1797 he married Charlotte Carpenter, an orphan of French extraction and ward of the Marquess of Downshire. In this letter, one of several written in the months preceding their marriage, Scott writes to Charlotte of his future financial prospects.

F2 Abbotsford

A letter to James Ballantyne, 12 May 1811, in which Scott announces his hope of buying two pieces of ground 'sufficient for a cottage and a few fields . . . a mile of the beautiful turn of Tweed above Gala-foot'. The phrase 'I must have recourse to my pen to make the matter easy' shows the close connection between Scott's profits and his property.

F3 Forestry

A letter from William Laidlaw, Scott's steward at Abbotsford, 27 November 1825, discussing the new planting of oaks on the Abbotsford estate. Scott took a passionate interest in the development of the property; there are frequent references to forestry in his *Journal*, and he reviewed R. Monteath's *The Forester's Guide* in the *Quarterly Review*, 1827.

F4 William Withers

A letter to Sir Walter Scott, Bart., exposing certain fundamental errors in his late essay on planting, and containing observations on the pruning and thinning of woods, and maxims for profitable planting. London, 1828.

With an inscription to Scott from the author.

F5 Washington Irving

Irving greatly admired Scott and visited him at Abbotsford in 1817. In this letter of 15 August 1820, he encloses a dedication copy of the second volume of his *Sketch Book*.

F6 Maria Edgeworth

A letter from the Irish novelist, 11 October 1824, in which she acknowledges a description by Sir Walter of the fashionable summer visitors to Abbotsford: '. . . I wish I had been by to see Rank and Wealth fighting it out, and you sitting by not to judge the prize with your innocent look which I never see without laughing internally. . . '

F7 Turner

A letter from J. M. W. Turner, 20 April 1831. He had been commissioned to make a series of illustrations of the *Poems*, and discusses the travel arrangements for a proposed visit to Abbotsford.

F8 James Hogg

Familiar Anecdotes of Sir Walter Scott. New-York, 1834.

The first edition of Hogg's short memoir, published in Glasgow later in the same year as *The Domestic Manners and Private Life of Sir Walter Scott*. The book gave deep offence to Lockhart and other members of the family.

F9 William Dalgleish

Anecdotes of Scott written by his valet in later years, William Dalgleish. This is a collection of characteristic domestic reminiscences, written in a vigorous and engaging phonetic spelling.

F10 Sir William Allan

Water-colour of Abbotsford, seen through the gateway.

Lent by the National Gallery of Scotland

F11 Sir William Allan

Water-colour of the library at Abbotsford. Lent by the National Gallery of Scotland

Allan visited Abbotsford for several weeks before Scott's death, and made a series of water-colours which were later engraved for Lockhart's *Life*. The view of the library shows the bust of Shakespeare at the far end, the silver urn which Byron gave to Scott, and the portrait of Sir Walter's son above the fireplace.

F1

Since Miss Carpenter has forbid my seeing
her for the present, I am willing to encour even the
hazard of her displeasure by intruding upon her in
this manner — My anxiety which is greater than I
can find words to express leads me to risque
what I am sure if you could but know my present
would not make you very — very angry — Gladly would
I have come to Carlisle tomorrow & returned here to dinner
but dearly as I love my friend I would ever sacri-
fice my own personal gratification to follow the line
of conduct which is most agreeable to her. I likewise wish to enter more particularly into the circumstances of my situation which I should most heartily
disdain myself were I capable of concealing or mis-
representing to you — Being only the second brother
of a large family you will easily conceive that tho
my father is a man in easy circumstances, my
success in life must depend upon my own exertions
this I have been always taught to expect and far
from considering it as a hardship, my feelings on

Dear Walter

I am truly sorry to write what will give you pain to read but an event has taken place which in a worldly point of view has carried away a most serious proportion of my worldly goods. This is the sudden and most unexpected Bankruptcy of Constable and Company here and their Agents and correspondents Hurst and Robinson in London both within these three weeks accounted the largest houses in London & Edinburgh & the[y] were safe. They had in their hands many engagements of mine for which I have wrought hard and will now not only not get a farthing but be obliged to pay back the cash I have received. How these affairs will turn out is uncertain but I look to be a great loser and may perhaps be so further than I at present calculate. It is hard at my time of life But as every body here is enclined to give me time I must hope that I will make a good fight I am not apprehensive of any body losing a penny and I trust with good management I may even save my land though it will be by reducing my scale of expense very much But I would give up much rather than part with Abbotsford and as James provisions are carefully secured on and I have some funds to bring about

G4 (detail)

CASE G

THE CRASH

G1 Contract of Co-Partnery

Lent by the Scott Bicentenary Exhibition Trustees

An agreement between Walter Scott, Principal Clerk of Session, James Ballantyne, Printer, and John Ballantyne, Publisher, in which they agree to act in co-partnership in the publishing business of John Ballantyne and Co., for seven years from 19 July 1809. A capital stock of £1,000 is specified (Scott providing half), and formal arrangements are made for the conduct of business. Scott also made a similar agreement with James Ballantyne for the printing business, involving a capital of £6,000.

G2 Scott and the Ballantynes

A collection of bills drawn by the Ballantynes, with Scott's signatures of acceptance. The history of these financial negotiations is a complicated one, but these bills indicate something of the scale of the transactions.

G3 Letter to Captain Walter Scott

A letter to his son, 26 January 1826, in which Sir Walter reports that 'an event has taken place which in the worldly point of view has carried away a most serious proportion of my worldly goods. This is the sudden and most unexpected Bankruptcy of Constable and Company here and their Agents and correspondents Hurst and Robinson in London. . . .'

G4 Letter to Lockhart

A letter to his son-in-law, 20 January 1826, discussing the financial difficulties and justifying his involvement in the commercial negotiations.

G5 The Creditors' Minutes

A minute of a meeting of Sir Walter's admiring and accommodating creditors at which they agreed to offer the library and plenishings of Abbotsford in acknowledgement 'for the unparalleled and most successful exertions he has made, and continues to make for them', 17 December 1830.

G6 Letter to Cadell

One of the long series of letters from Scott to Robert Cadell, the skilled publisher of his later works and of the *Magnum* edition. In this letter written from the Bay of Naples, 18 December 1831, Scott writes of his plans for a new novel, 'The Siege of Malta', which was never completed or published, and speaks of the expenses of his final journey in search of health. The letter was slit to be fumigated as a precaution against the plague, and is badly water-stained.

G7 Travelling Case

The leather dispatch-box which carried manuscripts between 'Walter Scott Esquire Sheriff of Selkirkshire' and 'James Ballantyne & Co. Printers Edinburgh'.

CASE H
LAST YEARS

H1   The Life of Napoleon Buonaparte,
Emperor of the French. With a preliminary view of the French Revolution. By the author of 'Waverley', &c. 9 vol. Edinburgh, 1827.

Projected in 1825 as the first volume of Constable's Miscellany but far outgrowing this intention, the *Life* was one of Scott's main preoccupations during the early months of financial disaster. His attempts to conceal his personal and national prejudices were unsuccessful, and the work was deeply resented in France. Goethe saw its real value as a document of English history in the light it shed on the British attitude to European affairs.

H2   Duke of Wellington
Scott made a diligent study of the available documents and anecdotes when preparing his *Life of Napoleon*. Amongst those he consulted was the Duke of Wellington, whose characteristically brief letter of 2 July 1827 acknowledging the published volumes is here displayed.

H3   Goethe
A letter to Scott from Goethe, the first of an elevated but sincere exchange of expressions of mutual admiration which took place in 1827. Scott had published his translation of *Goetz von Berlichingen* in 1799, but remarked to its author nearly thirty years later that he had forgotten 'that it is necessary not only to be acquainted with a work of genius but to be well acquainted with the language— before we attempt to communicate its beauty to others'.

H4   'The Great Unknown' Revealed
An account of the first Edinburgh Theatrical Fund Dinner, held at Edinburgh, on Friday 23d February 1827; containing a correct and authentic report of the speeches; which include among other interesting matter, the first public avowal, by Sir Walter Scott, of being the author of the Waverley Novels. Edinburgh, 1827.
The first public avowal of what had long been an open secret.

H5   John Leycester Adolphus
Letters to Richard Heber, Esq., containing critical remarks on the series of novels beginning with 'Waverley', and an attempt to ascertain their author. London, 1821.

J. L. Adolphus (1795–1862) had graduated from Oxford and was about to be called to the Bar when he published the *Letters*, anonymously, in 1821. By that time few people in Great Britain doubted that Scott was the author of the Waverley Novels, and on the Continent

they were normally published under his name. The cogent arguments with which Adolphus supported his identification of Scott with 'the Author of *Waverley*', based on the similarities of thought, language, characters and historical background in the poems and novels, not only proved his point but embodied some of the best criticism of Scott's works ever written.

H6   Chronicles of the Canongate
By the author of 'Waverley', &c. 2 vol. Edinburgh, 1827. (Worthington 20).

The introduction is signed Walter Scott, and in it the authorship of the Waverley Novels is acknowledged—the first time Scott's name had appeared in an authorised edition of the novels.

H7   The Keepsake for 1829
London, 1828.

Charles Heath, engraver and publisher of the annual, asked Scott in 1828 to become its editor. Scott declined but contributed three tales 'My Aunt Margaret's Mirror,' 'The Tapestried Chamber' and 'The Laird's Jock' to the issue for 1829, and his play 'The House of Aspen' to the issue for 1830.

H8   Tales of a Grandfather
Stories taken from Scottish history. Humbly inscribed to Hugh Littlejohn, Esq. 3 vol. Edinburgh, 1828.

Written for John Hugh Lockhart, the much-loved grandson whose delicate health caused Scott so much anxiety and sorrow until his death in 1831 at the age of nine. It fulfils Scott's hope that he might 'make if possible a book that a child will understand yet a man will feel some temptation to peruse should he chance to take it up'.

H9   History of Scotland
The corrected galley-proofs of Scott's *History of Scotland*, one of the many miscellaneous compositions of his later years undertaken mainly to set against the debit account. It met with an indifferent critical reception.

H10   The Doom of Devorgoil
A melodrama. Auchindrane; or, the Ayrshire tragedy. Edinburgh, 1830.

Scott's own plays had little of the success of the 'Terryfications' of his novels. He wrote *The Doom of Devorgoil* for Terry in 1817–18, but though Terry worked hard to fit it for the stage, it was neither performed nor published at that time. In 1830 Scott brought it to light again to play its part in his struggle to reduce his debts, and it was published along with the recently written *Auchindrane*.

H11   Daniel Terry
Terry, the actor, theatrical manager, and adapter of Scott's novels for the stage, modelled his handwriting on Sir Walter Scott's. In this letter of 11 February 1818 he sends detailed criticisms of Scott's drama *The Doom of Devorgoil*. Shown alongside for comparison is a letter from Scott to Terry, 4 May 1818.

H12   Letters of Demonology and Witchcraft,
Addressed to J. G. Lockhart, Esq. London, 1830.

Written for Murray's Family Library, one of the projects of the Society for the Diffusion of Useful Knowledge. Scott's interest in superstitions and the supernatural made the subject a congenial one, but the *Letters* were undertaken after his first stroke in February 1830, at a time when he was already fully engaged with the Magnum Opus and the fourth series of *Tales of a Grandfather*, and he found the additional work 'a task to which my poverty and not my will consents'.

H13   Harriet Siddons
A letter from Mrs Harriet Siddons on 29 March 1830 (daughter-in-law of the more famous Sarah) asking Scott to write an epilogue for her farewell benefit performance. A page of Scott's reply is also shown, with his verses to be spoken at the end of *The Provok'd Husband* by Vanbrugh and Colley Cibber.

H14   Private Letters of the 17th Century
Late in 1831, in his never-ceasing, anxious preoccupation with the payment of his creditors, Scott's thoughts turned to the series of letters he had started to write, with some collaboration from Lady Louisa Stuart, in 1821. They were a description of life at the Court of James I, and purported to have come from the papers of a noble family. Lockhart and Ballantyne persuaded Scott to abandon the letters in favour of a novel, and he turned instead to *The Fortunes of Nigel* with its similar setting. Some copies of the *Letters* were printed, but they were not published either in 1821 or in 1831, when Scott revived the project, and only two copies are known to have survived. 'A magnificent fragment' was the description given by its editor when it was reprinted in 1948.

H15   The Last Voyage
After visiting Malta, Scott moved on to Naples, where he was received by his son Charles. Charles's letter to his sister Sophia Lockhart gives a vivid description of their father's distressing condition.

H16   Death of Scott
A notification to a country neighbour of Sir Walter Scott's death on 21 September 1832, signed by his son Walter, who succeeded him in the baronetcy of Scott of Abbotsford.

CASE J
TRANSLATIONS AND INFLUENCE

Translations of Scott's poetry and novels appeared in many European countries, sometimes almost as soon as they were published in this country. Publishers abroad had no doubts of the identity of 'the Author of *Waverley*' and attributed the novels to Scott long before he acknowledged them in the British editions.

J1   Guy Mannering
Astrologue, nouvelle écossaise. Traduit de l'anglais, sur la troisième édition. Par J. Martin. 4 vol. Paris, 1816.

The first French translation from the Waverley Novels. From 1816, rather slowly until 1820, then increasingly until the end of Scott's life, translations spread the enjoyment of the novels among the mass of readers in France who could not read them in English.

J2   Les Puritians d'Ecosse, et le Nain mystérieux
Contes de mon hôte, recueillis et mis au jour par Jedediah Cleishbotham. 4 vol. Paris, 1817.

The first translation by A. J. B. Defauconpret who became the regular translator of the novels. His translations, collected as the *Œuvres complètes* ran to several editions before 1840, and sold millions of copies.

J3   Schottische Lieder und Balladen
Übersetzt von Henriette Schubart. Leipzig, 1817.

Henriette Schubart who translated this selection from the *Minstrelsy* was the sister-in-law of Clemens Brentano, editor along with Achim von Arnim of the outstanding collection of German folk poetry *Des Knaben Wunderhorn*, 1806. In a review of this translation Arnim recalled that his acquaintance with the *Minstreley* during a visit to England in 1803 was one of the important influences on the *Wunderhorn*. Henriette Schubart presented a copy of her translation to Scott in April 1817.

J4   Der Pirat
Aus dem Englischen des Walter Scott übersetzt von S. H. Spiker. 3 Bd. Berlin, 1822.

German translations of the novels began to make their appearance only a year or two after the French and met with similar success. This translation by Spiker, the Librarian to the King of Prussia, was one of four German versions of *The Pirate* announced for the same year.

J8

ROBBERT ROODHAAR.

DOOR

SIR WALTER SCOTT.

Uit het Engelsch.

TWEEDE DEEL.

Te GRONINGEN, bij
W. VAN BOEKEREN.
MDCCCXXVI.

J5   Kenilworth
Volgarizzato dal Professore Gaetano Barbieri. 4 tom. Milano, 1821.

The first of the collection 'Romanzi Storici di Walter Scott' edited by Barbieri, himself the translator of several of Scott's novels and author of a version of *Kenilworth* for the Italian stage.

J6   L'officiale di Fortuna
Episodio delle guerre di Montrose. Traduzione di Vincenzo Lancetti. 2 tom. Milano, 1822.

A translation of *A Legend of Montrose* for the series 'Romanzi Storici.' Lancetti was the author of *Cabrino Fondulo*, one of the many historical novels to show Scott's influence in Italy.

J7   El Anticuario
Puesto en Castellano. 5 tom. Barcelona, 1834.

Scott's recognition was somewhat slow in Spain. The first Spanish translation was *Ivanhoe*, published in London in 1825. In the later 1820s and early 1830s most of the novels and poems were translated and published in Spain.

J8   Robbert Roodhaar
3 vol. Groningen, 1826.

Dutch translations of *Ivanhoe* and *Waverley* in 1824 were quickly followed by most of the other novels.

J9   Waverley
Eller Skottland för 80 ar sedan. 4 vol, Stockholm, 1824–1826.

Beginning with *Ivanhoe* in 1821, most of Scott's novels were translated into Swedish during the 1820s. This translation of *Waverley* was by Jakob Ekelund.

It was inevitable that Scott's success with the historical novel should result in a host of imitations both in this country and abroad. He saw the first of the long line of followers and summed up the difference between their hastily acquired and insufficiently assimilated knowledge and the depth and range of his own historical learning—'They may do their fooling with better grace; but I, like Sir Andrew Aguecheek, do it more natural'. The achievements of his successors down to the present day in the main support his judgement, though there are brilliant exceptions.

J10   Alfred de Vigny

Cinq Mars, ou une Conjuration sous Louis XIII. 2 tom. Paris, 1826.

Lent by Mrs Maxwell-Scott of Abbotsford

Vigny, in common with many of the French Romantics, was much influenced by Scott in his early work. *Cinq Mars*, his first novel, shows many resemblances to *Quentin Durward*, but it also illustrates Vigny's preference for giving greater prominence to his historical characters than Scott normally did. This copy was given by Vigny to Scott after their meeting in Paris in 1826.

J11   Victor Hugo

Han d'Islande. Paris, 1823.

Lent by Mrs Maxwell-Scott of Abbotsford

Hugo's first novel, written under the influence of his youthful admiration for Scott, but bearing more resemblance to the horror novels of the Gothic romancers. *Notre Dame*, published eight years later, still reveals traces of Scott's methods, but has become the vehicle for Hugo's powerful imagination, brilliant descriptive gifts, and love of the gigantic, the mysterious and the grotesque.

J12   Alexandre Dumas

Le Comte de Monte-Christo. 18 vol. Paris, 1845.

Dumas made use of the Waverley Novels in several of his plays, including *Le Laird de Dumbicky*, which owes its title, but nothing else, to *The Heart of Mid-Lothian*. When he turned to novel-writing, he was to become Scott's greatest rival in popularity, his inferior in character-drawing and the integration of the historical background, but his master in the drama and excitement of the narrative.

J13   Complément de Walter Scott

Guide pittoresque du voyageur en Ecosse, Paris, 1838.

'Avant la publication de *Waverley*, l'Ecosse n'était guère connue en Europe que sous le rapport des événements qui s'y passerent en 1715 et en 1745.' Thus opens the introduction to this illustrated guidebook, combining a thorough and detailed directory with numerous engravings of historic or romantic interest for the tourist.

J14   Alessandro Manzoni

I Promessi Sposi. Storia milanese del secoló XVII. Milano, 1840.

The first illustrated edition, a revision of the original version published in 1827. Manzoni took the idea of the historical novel from Scott, but in his hands it became a vehicle for the expression of complex philosophic, religious and sociological beliefs.

J15   Edward Bulwer-Lytton

The Last Days of Pompeii. 3 vol. London, 1834.

J16   Nathaniel Hawthorne

The Scarlet Letter. Boston, 1850.

J17   William Makepeace Thackeray

The History of Henry Esmond, Esq. 3 vol. London, 1832.

J18   Robert Louis Stevenson

The Black Arrow. London, 1888.

One or two of the more notable historical novels in the English language which show how the pattern set by Scott has been modified to suit the gifts of his successors.

J19   Edinburgh Review

Or Critical Journal. May 1828.

Scott's influence was strong not only on the writing of fiction but of history. This number of the *Edinburgh Review* contains Macaulay's article on History, in which, as G. M. Trevelyan says in his essay on the Influence of Sir Walter Scott on History, in *An Autobiography and other Essays* (1949), 'he avows the ambition to write serious history with the colour, variety, and human detail of Scott, and to show in professional histories, as Sir Walter had done in his novels, the social and economic causes of political events, which older historians had treated *in vacuo*'.

J20   Thomas Carlyle

Critical and Miscellaneous Essays. vol. 4. London, 1839.

In his review of Lockhart's *Life of Scott*, written for the *London and Westminster Review* of January 1838 and reprinted in this collection of essays, Carlyle (in a critical tradition deriving from Jeffrey) castigated the Waverley Novels as superficial and lacking in serious purpose, but recognised their importance for the writing of history in showing 'that the by-gone ages of the world were actually filled by living men, not by protocols, state-papers, controversies, and abstractions of men'.

1771   Born on 15 August at College Wynd, Edinburgh, son of Walter Scott, W.S.

1773   Illness resulting in permanent lameness

1773–6   Lives with his grandparents at Sandy-Knowe near Kelso, and visits London and Bath with his aunt, Janet Scott

1776   Returns to the family home at George Square, Edinburgh

1779–83   Attends the High School in Edinburgh

1783   Spends some months in Kelso and meets James Ballantyne

1785–6   Attends classes in Latin, Greek and Logic at Edinburgh University

1786   Serious illness and convalescence, spent partly in Kelso. Begins apprenticeship as Writer to the Signet with his father

1789–92   Attends law classes at Edinburgh University

1792   Admitted to the Faculty of Advocates. Falls in love with Williamina Belsches

1795   Appointed a Curator of the Advocates' Library

1796   Loses Williamina Belsches, who marries Sir William Forbes

        The Chase, and William and Helen, translated from Bürger

1797   Becomes Quartermaster of the Royal Edinburgh Light Dragoons
Marries Charlotte Carpenter

1798   Sets up house in Castle Street

1799   Death of his father. Rents a country cottage at Lasswade

        Appointed Sheriff of Selkirkshire

1800   *Goetz of Berlichingen*, translated from Goethe. *The Eve of Saint John*

1802–3   *Minstrelsy of the Scottish Border*, 3 vol.

1804   Moves country home from Lasswade to Ashestiel

        Edits *Sir Tristrem*, by Thomas the Rhymer

1805   Goes into partnership with James Ballantyne, who moved his printing-house from Kelso to Edinburgh in 1802

        The Lay of the Last Minstrel

1806   Appointed a Principal Clerk of the Court of Session

Ballads and Lyrical Pieces

1808   Quarrels with Constable and starts a publishing-house with John Ballantyne

Marmion; edits *The Works of Dryden* and Joseph Strutt's *Queenhoo Hall*

1809   Edits *A Collection of Scarce and Valuable Tracts* (Somers Tracts), 13 vol. 1809–15

1810   *The Lady of the Lake;* edits *English Minstrelsy,* and *The Poetical Works of Anna Seward*

1811   Buys the farm which becomes Abbotsford

The Vision of Don Roderick; edits *Secret History of the Court of James I,* and Walpole's *Castle of Otranto*

1812   Removes from Ashestiel to Abbotsford

1813   Declines Poet Laureateship. Publishing firm of John Ballantyne wound up

Rokeby; The Bridal of Triermain

1814   Voyage to Orkney, Shetland and the Hebrides aboard the Lighthouse Yacht

Waverley; edits *The Works of Jonathan Swift*

1815   Visits London, Paris and Waterloo

The Lord of the Isles; Guy Mannering; The Field of Waterloo; edits *Memorie of the Somervilles*

1816   *The Antiquary; Tales of my Landlord* (*The Black Dwarf* and *Old Mortality*); *Paul's Letters to his Kinsfolk*

1817   First attack of cramp in the stomach. Purchases more land adjoining Abbotsford

Harold the Dauntless; Introduction to *The Border Antiquities*

1818   Brings to light the Regalia of Scotland. Is offered and accepts Baronetcy

Rob Roy; Tales of my Landlord, second series (*The Heart of Mid-Lothian*)

1819   Further attacks of cramp. His mother dies

Tales of my Landlord, third series (*The Bride of Lammermoor* and *A Legend of Montrose*)

1820   Visits London and sits to Chantrey and Lawrence. Marriage of his daughter Sophia to J. G. Lockhart

Ivanhoe; The Monastery; The Abbot

1821   Attends the Coronation of George IV

Kenilworth; Lives of the Novelists (prefaces to Ballantyne's Novelist's Library) 1821–4

1822   Organizes the King's visit to Scotland

The Pirate; Halidon Hill; The Fortunes of Nigel; Peveril of the Peak

1823   Suffers his first stroke. Founds and becomes President of the Bannatyne Club

Quentin Durward

1824   *St. Ronan's Well; Redgauntlet*

1825   Marriage of his son Walter to Jane Jobson. Visits Ireland and the Lake District

Tales of the Crusaders (The Betrothed and The Talisman)

1826   Financial crash. Leaves 39 Castle Street. Death of Lady Scott. Visit to London and Paris

Woodstock

1827   Public acknowledgement of the authorship of the Waverley Novels

Life of Napoleon Buonaparte; Chronicles of the Canongate (The Highland Widow, The Two Drovers and The Surgeon's Daughter)

1828   Visit to London

Tales of a Grandfather, first series; *Chronicles of the Canongate*, second series (*The Fair Maid of Perth*); 'My Aunt Margaret's Mirror', 'The Tapestried Chamber' and 'Death of the Laird's Jock' contributed to *The Keepsake* for 1829

1829   *Tales of a Grandfather*, second series; *Anne of Geierstein*; 'The House of Aspen', contributed to *The Keepsake* for 1830; The 'Magnum Opus' edition of the Waverley novels, with introductions and notes. 48 vols. 1829–33

1830   Suffers strokes in February and November. Resigns Clerkship of the Court of Session

Tales of a Grandfather, third series; *History of Scotland*, vols 1 & 2; *The Doom of Devorgoil and Auchindrane; Letters on Demonology and Witchcraft*

1831   Suffers further stroke in May. Sails on H.M.S. BARHAM to Malta and Naples

Tales of a Grandfather, fourth series

1832   Residence at Naples, return by the Rhine, and death at Abbotsford on 21 September

Tales of my Landlord, fourth series (*Count Robert of Paris* and *Castle Dangerous*)

Novels

There are innumerable editions of the best-known Waverley Novels and many complete editions of the whole set, of which Scott's own 'Magnum Opus' (48 vols, 1829–33), the Dryburgh Edition (25 vols, 1892–4), and the Border Edition (48 vols, 1892–4), edited by Andrew Lang, provide satisfactory texts. Many recent editions and translations of selected novels are in print. Lockhart edited the *Miscellaneous Prose Works* (28 vols, 1834–6), which contain many interesting shorter writings.

Poems

The Poetical Works of Sir Walter Scott, ed. J. Logie Robertson (1894 and many reprints) in the Oxford Standard Authors series is the most convenient modern edition.

Journal

The Journal of Sir Walter Scott, ed. J. G. Tait and W. M. Parker (3 vols, 1939–46 and 1 vol, 1950). A new edition by W. E. K. Anderson is in preparation.

Letters

The Letters of Sir Walter Scott, ed. H. J. C. Grierson (Centenary Edition, 12 vols, 1932–7) is full, but not comprehensive. An index is in preparation.

Biography

J. G. Lockhart, *Memoirs of the Life of Sir Walter Scott, Bart.* (7 vols, 1837–8, and many later editions) is basic: a new edition by John Cameron is in preparation. Several good modern lives, including John Buchan, *Sir Walter Scott* (1932) and H. J. C. Grierson, *Sir Walter Scott, Bart.* (1938). Ian Jack's British Council pamphlet, *Sir Walter Scott* (1958) is a good brief introduction with a select bibliography. Thomas Crawford, *Scott* (1965) is a good short critical and biographical study. Arthur Melville Clark, *Scott: The Formative Years* (1969), deals gracefully with his early life. Edgar Johnson, *Sir Walter Scott, The Great Unknown* (2 vols, 1970) is very full and "definitive".

Guides to more detailed study

James C. Corson's section on Scott in *The New Cambridge Bibliography of English Literature*, III (1969) 670–691, is a good start. His *Bibliography of Scott, 1797–1940* (1943) is indispensable. Greville Worthington, *A Bibliography of the Waverley Novels* (1930) discusses first editions. William Ruff, 'A Bibliography of the Poetical Works of Scott, 1796–1832' in *Edinburgh Bibliographical Society Transactions*, I (1938), and Gillian Dyson 'The MSS. and Proof Sheets of Scott's Waverley Novels', in the same journal, IV (1960), are standard.

Her Majesty The Queen 62; A14

Captain C. K. Adam of Blair-Adam 51–2

The Faculty of Advocates 82

His Grace the Duke of Buccleuch 5; A13

The Rt Hon. Lord Clyde 78

Dr James C. Corson A24, A30

Edinburgh City Museums 83

Edinburgh Public Libraries
7–9, 64, 72, 74, 78–81

Edinburgh University 73

Mr D. A. O. Edward 55

Sir Gregor MacGregor of MacGregor, Bt
68, 70

King's School, Canterbury E7

Mrs Patricia Maxwell-Scott of Abbotsford
11–15, 17–18, 76; A4–5, A19, E5,
J10–11

National Gallery of Scotland
2–4, 20–22, 53, 56–7, 80; D6, F10–11

National Library of Scotland
A–J *passim*

National Portrait Gallery, London
32–3, 35

Mr William Nichol 25

The Rt Hon. Lord Polwarth 19

Dr John Pym B1

Royal Scottish Academy 49

Scott Bicentenary Exhibition Trustees G1

Scottish National Portrait Gallery
7, 10, 16, 24, 26–31, 34, 36–48, 50,
60–61, 63, 66–7, 71, 75, 84

Mr George Scott-Moncrieff B6

The Signet Library C15

Dr David C. Simpson 6, 8, 59, 65, 69,
79–80

Speculative Society B4

Mr and Mrs Alan Stark 54

Mrs S. D. Wheeler-Carmichael 23

Acknowledgements

President
The Rt Hon. the Earl of Crawford and
Balcarres, KT

Planning Committee
The Rt Hon. Lord Clyde (Court of
Session); D. A. O. Edward (Faculty of
Advocates); ProfessorWilliam Beattie,
A. S. Bell (National Library of Scotland);
R. E. Hutchison (Scottish National
Portrait Gallery); W. E. K. Anderson,
John Reid, FRIBA, B. C. Skinner

Catalogue
W. E. K. Anderson, B. C. Skinner
(Portraits and Illustrations);
Marion P. Linton, A. S. Bell (*Editor*)
(Books and Manuscripts);
D. A. O. Edward (Buildings);
H. R. Trevor-Roper (Scott's Influence
Abroad)

Music and Sound
Martin J. Ellis, FRCO (Arrangement)
Cargilfield Chapel, Edinburgh (Organ)
Graham Melville Mason, Martin Mitchell
(Recording)
Ian Gilmour and Meta Forrest
(Scott Readings)
Craighall Recording Studios, Edinburgh
(Recording)
Reditune Limited, Jute Industries Limited,
Dundee (Equipment)
An Advocate; John M. Brown,
Robert W. Blackadder (Parliament House)
(Court-room Setting)

Exhibition Design
Ian G. Lindsay and Partners

Catalogue Design and Exhibition Graphics
Graham Duffy of Graphic Partners,
Edinburgh

Exhibition Managers
J. Gordon Brown and Robert Cairns

Catering
Mary A. Hogan

The Committee gratefully acknowledges
the generous financial support and
encouragement it has received from many
Scottish institutions and trusts.